Turkestan Reunion

Turkestan Reunion

ELEANOR HOLGATE LATTIMORE

Decorations by Eleanor Frances Lattimore
With a new foreword by Evelyn Stefansson Nef
and a biographical note by David Lattimore

KODANSHA INTERNATIONAL
New York · Tokyo · London

Kodansha America, Inc.
114 Fifth Avenue, New York, New York 10011, U.S.A.

Kodansha International Ltd.
17-14 Otowa 1-chome, Bunkyo-ku, Tokyo 112, Japan

Published in 1994 by Kodansha America, Inc.
by arrangement with The Eleanor Holgate Lattimore Trust.

First published in 1934 by The John Day Company, New York.

This is a Kodansha Globe book.

Library of Congress Cataloging-in-Publication Data
Lattimore, Eleanor Holgate, 1895-1970.
  Turkestan reunion / Eleanor Holgate Lattimore ; decorations by
Eleanor Frances Lattimore ; with a new foreword by Evelyn Stefansson
Nef and a biographical note by David Lattimore.
    p.   cm.—(Kodansha globe)
  Reprint of the 1975 ed. published by AMS Press, 1975.
  ISBN 1-56836-053-3
  1. Sinkiang Uighur Autonomous Region (China)—Description and
travel. 2. Siberia (Russia)—Description and travel. 3. Lattimore.
Eleanor Holgate, 1895-1970. I. Stefansson, Evelyn Schwartz Baird,
1913-   . II. Title. III. Series.
DS793.S62L28   1994
915.1'6'0441—dc20   94-40023

Printed in the United States of America

94 95 96 97 98   QP/F   10 9 8 7 6 5 4 3 2 1

"By George," he cried, "I wonder whether that's the real truth about East and West! That the gorgeous East offers everything needed for adventures except the man to enjoy them. It would explain the tradition of the Crusades uncommonly well. Perhaps that's what God meant by Europe and Asia. We dress the characters and they paint the scenery."

From *The Flying Inn* by G. K. Chesterton.

CONTENTS

Contents

FOREWORD
Evelyn Stefansson Nef

IN New York City, in 1939, I was the newest member of a large staff at the Polar Library of a famous Arctic explorer, Vilhjalmur Stefansson. One of my duties was to prepare lunch for the senior staff and for any visiting explorers or scientists who came to use the library and confer with Stef.

One day, Owen and Eleanor Lattimore arrived fresh from a recent Asian expedition. They were young, handsome, articulate, and experts in their field of Chinese and Mongolian human geography and history. As a young woman, Eleanor Holgate had become a teacher and youth worker and gone out to China—an adventurous thing to do in her time, to say the least. There she had taught and later became Secretary of the Peking Institute of Fine Arts. In China, she had met and married Owen Lattimore.

The luncheon recital of this pair of world travelers was packed with interesting, exotic facts and laced with enthusiasm and humor. I was deeply impressed by their seamless behavior as a couple, especially the neat, easy way they handed the floor to each other and the verbal counterpoint they developed as they enlarged and enhanced one another's narrative.

In 1941, I married Vilhjalmur Stefansson, and during the more than four decades that Eleanor shared Owen's life in travel and scholarhip, we and the Lattimores became a like-minded quartet. We were all travelers, Stef and I in the Arctic, Owen and Eleanor in Asia; we were all writers, researchers, and editors. Eleanor had a cheerful, lively intelligence, and I soon discovered that what Eleanor had accomplished in that conversation at lunch she also did in life. Using her excellent mind, delicate and precise powers of observation, and social gifts, she not merely complimented Owen's range but also extended it. And she did it easily, with good humor and pleasure.

Eleanor also had a discerning eye for discovering beautiful things, an awareness of color, texture, and line which any good artist would envy. In the way she dressed and in her various houses, she used those skills to create a distinctive, distinguished look. We summered together at our farm in Vermont and spent many Christmas vacations in their beautiful house in Towson, Maryland.

Christmas at the Lattimores was a joyous time. The house would be festively decorated, the dinner table set with unusual and colorful linen, plates, silver, and candles collected from the far corners of the globe, all chosen with Eleanor's unerring eye—and combined in surprising and always pleasing ways. David, their son, would be home from Harvard (he is now a professor of Chinese at Brown University). The Dilowa Hutuktu, a Mongol priest high in the Buddhist church, a refugee from communist Mongolia, was always present; he spoke not a word of English but could manage to smile and shed his benign sweetness on the assemblage. Owen, in a long Mongol robe (and probably barefoot) managed the drinks, the carving, and the singing. Eleanor presided over all, orchestrating the exchange of gifts and seating us and other guests at the huge, round Chinese black lacquer table that was surrounded by antique Hitchcock chairs for the holiday dinner.

One Christmas, her gift to me was a dozen paperwhite narcissus bulbs and a handsome bowl in which to grow them. Odd and interesting plants would fill the house the year round, but from Thanksgiving on there were always the paperwhites, including those in flower, which perfumed the living room. Every year since, although I lack Eleanor's green thumb, I follow her example, buying, planting, and cultivating the bulbs from Thanksgiving through Christmas. It has become a loving memorial ritual.

Stef and Owen shared anthropological interests and spent much time comparing Eskimo and Mongol mores and linguistics. Eleanor shared her design and furnishing know-how with me, and we went to country auctions, hunted for antiques, and made or found inexpensive, smart clothes. Eleanor had the gift of humanizing and beautifying whatever place she found herself in, whether it was a Mongolian yurt, a hotel room in Yugoslavia, or a stone house in Yorkshire. She became my role model and best friend, and she held that place until her untimely death in 1970.

Eleanor's charm and sense of herself enabled her to befriend almost everybody. In traveling, she had a willingness, nay, a pleasure, in roughing it without complaint. A born problem-solver, she could find a job for a needy person, beg clothes and cash income for the Mongol refugees from communism that worked with Owen at Johns Hopkins University, and remember her friends with small but perfectly selected little presents.

Our friendship, which was close before the nightmare era when Senator McCarthy tried to label Owen a "Communist" and a "traitor," became even more intimate during a time when many fairweather friends disappeared. The Lattimores learned then who their real friends were. They lost some, but made new and lasting ones as well. Eleanor was the heroine of that time in their lives. The false accusation of *spy* was made while Owen was in Afghanistan on a special mission for the United Nations; by the time he returned, she had found appropriate lawyers, provided them with the records they needed for his defense, and galvanized friends to help. When the pressures closed in, it was she who took over many of the chores of handling the press, protecting him where she could, and urging him to continue with his writing and Mongol studies.

I remember her powers of organization, her determination, her almost physical preservation of her family's sanity and life. William Rogers who worked closely with her describes this in his memoir: "Through the whole trying struggle, she it was who drudged. And she it was who shielded. . . . And she did so cheerfully, almost radiant in her conviction that what she was doing, though it may have been endlessly revolting, was also infinitely important. In this, she inspired us all." She became his protector and his scribe—the two co-authored a book about this struggle, *Ordeal by Slander* —and, I believe, paid the price for it in her health.

Fortune gave Eleanor opportunity to play many roles in her rich life. How lucky she was to possess both the mental and physical resources with which to perform them splendidly. Teacher, writer, editor, researcher, traveler, wife, homemaker, mother, and grandmother —these words give no hint of the good spirit that accompanied each activity she threw herself into, the contagious ebullient pleasure she discovered in interesting people, good books, and beautiful things, the range and efficiency of Eleanor the problem-solver, or her sensitivity as a comforter. To me she was a rare and beautiful happening, a true friend, whose spirit will live at least as long as I do—since I agree with the primitive Eskimo belief that each spirit lives on in another person for one more generation before it disappears.

This first book of Eleanor's is about traveling in a distant place where few foreigners and no women had penetrated before. Some years back, in celebrating the fiftieth anniversary of the Society of Woman Geographers, a national organization women formed at the time when they were excluded from the all-male Explorers Club, I delved into the early history of the organization and there found Eleanor Lattimore and her journeys. I was charmed, and you will be too with this entrancing narrative.

INTRODUCTION TO THE 1975 EDITION

WHEN Eleanor and I first met in Peking in 1925, she was already a more experienced traveller than I. She had travelled with pack-horses in the Pacific Northwest, and had done a lot of camping while doing youth work with the Y.M.C.A. toward the end of the First World War. She and another girl had taken a walking trip in Norway, while waiting for word that they would be granted visas to travel via Siberia to China. That long journey by rail, sleeping "hard," that is, on wooden shelves rather than in "soft" sleeping berths, was a good initiation for the rail journey through Siberia, made this time alone, and described at the beginning of *Turkestan Reunion*.

During the months that we knew each other before our marriage, Eleanor and I, like so many of the young Americans and Europeans in Peking, especially the Americans, did a great deal of weekend walking in the Western Hills. We carried camp beds with us, packed on donkeys, and slept in the courtyards of Buddhist temples. What turned out to be extremely important was that Eleanor was already an expert in the art of packing, an art which I never mastered. My way was to spread out what I was going to take, estimate how many boxes and how many bags would be needed, and then stuff everything in. Eleanor could do a mental calculation, counting the stages of the journey and dividing things up with beautiful accuracy so that at the right stage of the journey the right box or bag would be opened up, and the right things would be there. That is a great deal more difficult than it sounds, especially when the planning has to be done to fit packing-units of a size that can be either fitted and stacked in a cart, without tumbling all over each other, or, in lower country, divided into half-loads which can be lashed on each side of a pack-horse. For several of the really high passes where the horses, weakened and short of breath, had to be led over unloaded, the packs were shifted to grunting, sure-footed, imperturbable yaks.

Eleanor and I debated a long time about this journey. I had been planning it for months before we met. I had read everything I could in preparation, had made the necessary contacts in advance with the merchants of the caravan trade who would eventually hand me over to the men who did the actual caravan travel, and had sketched out a route through Mongolia to Sinkiang (the "Turkestan" of this book), that would be "new": that is, it would repeat as little as possible of the routes of the great names like Huc and Gabet, Ney Elias and Sir Francis Younghusband and Douglas Carruthers, or Prjevalskii and the other legendary Russians. Once in Sinkiang, the travelling would be along known routes. The only novelty would be that, although there were British and Russian consuls (first Tsarist and later Soviet) as well as Swedish and British Protestant missionaries and German Catholics in this province, it had hardly been visited by foreign travellers for many years. Moreover, Eleanor would be the first American woman to visit this remote province and to travel all the way overland from Peking to India.

Eleanor very much wanted to journey all the way with me but I thought better not. The times were bad for travel (though not in Sinkiang), and getting worse. The great "Northern Expedition" of the United Front of the Kuomintang and the Chinese Communists was building up. Chiang Kai-shek had yet to turn against his Communist allies, and though Eleanor and I were politically too ignorant to understand what was really going on, we yet could see that waves of what might be called secondary civil warfare were spreading in North China. Some of these especially endangered lines of communication and travel along the Inner Mongolian frontier. Under such uncertain conditions there might well be trouble in persuading the caravan men to take a woman along. A man travelling alone, especially a Chinese-speaking man, would be much less conspicuous and less likely to attract the attention of bandits or disorganized and demoralized soldiery.

So it was decided that I should go alone as far as Sinkiang. Once there, we knew that there was a radio station at Urumchi. I could send a message to Eleanor. She could take the "safer" journey by rail through Siberia. I could go some 400 miles into Soviet territory to meet her at Semipalatinsk, the rail-head of the then uncompleted Turk-Sib (Turkestan-Siberian) railway, and we could then return to Sinkiang and get on with our travelling.

In writing of Eleanor's journey I called it "safer." Irony, and on my part a proper modesty, demand the quotation marks. During the few weeks before deciding that we would actually go to Tientsin and get married —although it was undoubtedly risky and perhaps totally crazy—I remember daydreaming of the romance of camp life in Central Asia. I would be coming down from the forested slopes of a mountain, having shot a roebuck or something else good to eat, and there in a high, flower-speckled alpine meadow would be our little blue *maik-han*, the tent used by Chinese caravan men and by Mongols when they are travelling fast and do not want to spend time on putting up their more solid, round, felt tents. It would be fine weather, and the fire would be made outside the tent. The little woman would be tending it, and from quite a distance I would see that always wonderful smile of hers, and from a little nearer the expression in her eyes, greeting her food-providing, road-finding, he-man husband. Proper male chauvinist pig stuff, it sounds, although in truth it did work out that way quite a number of times.

It also worked out, however, that from the very beginning she had more than her share of the difficulties and dangers. Her description of finding her way across Siberia, especially the 400 miles or so of travelling by horse-drawn sled after leaving the railway, shows that she was also the better road-finder. How she did it, I don't know. In speaking and writing English Eleanor had grace and elegance, a natural distinction of style, but she had difficulty with other languages. Her Chinese was never more than rudimentary, and her Russian, as she good-humouredly shows, was at the level of the phrasebook and the traveller's pocket dictionary.

And yet I do know how she did it. Eleanor radiated a warm humanity to which people responded. She never begged for help, was never arch or coy, never played the helpless woman. In our long years together, I saw Eleanor in a good many tough spots; and the tougher the spot, the more she looked interested, never daunted. Her humanity was of the kind that was always helping others—often strangers—and always effectively, because she never failed to size up a situation and see what had to be done. Because people sensed this quality in her, they always helped her. All of this returns to the point of irony. Instead of being the one who met her at rail-head, took charge of her, and escorted her gallantly and protectively on the difficult sled journey, it was I who sat helpless at the Soviet frontier (Eleanor's account explains the visa trouble), while she coped with the situation, made the journey, found me and rescued me from my baffled despondency.

Things like that happened a number of times in our life together, the most important when the late Joseph McCarthy accused me—the man who had been refused a Soviet visa—of being "the chief Soviet agent in America." I was in Afghanistan when the sensational accusation went out over the air-waves of the world. McCarthy had a genius for publicity. He firmly established the legend that I had to drop everything and rush home in a panic; the truth is that I insisted on staying in Afghanistan until the agreed date for the end of my mission (which was for the United Nations). By the time I got home, Eleanor had once more "coped." With the aid of the most generous, as well as the most politically fearless law firm in Washington—Arnold, Fortas and Porter—a successful defense was already being shaped up, although it would take about five years.

One or two stories remain to be told. I want to add to what Eleanor says about "Moses" on pages 67–68, principally because I have become sensitive to the fear that people might think that Eleanor and I had some kind of colonial, white-man-superiority in calling a Chinese servant by a name like that. Moses—his name was Li Pao-shu—was born in Hopei province, near the Shantung border. In 1900, the year of the Boxer Rebellion, things were pretty grim in that part of China. There were several brothers in the family, and Moses, the youngest, was only in his teens. The family made a move which must have been made by many a Chinese family in the recurrent peasant rebellions throughout Chinese history. Moses was sent to join the Boxers, because being so young he would be better able to keep out of serious fighting, while at the same time the fact that one brother was with the Boxers would help the others to dodge joining the Boxers, without implicating the family as "anti-Boxer."

After the suppression of the Boxers there was a hunt for scapegoats, and as it is well known that the relatively innocent make handy scapegoats it was thought wise to get Moses out of the way. That was how he came to go to South Africa as an indentured labourer—a man who signed away his freedom for a term of years at a fixed rate of pay, without the right to organize or strike, but with the right to be sent home at the end of his term. When Moses got to South Africa, it was discovered that he was below the legal age for working underground as a miner (I forget whether it was a diamond mine or a gold mine), and so was assigned to odd-job work above-ground. It was this that gave him an opportunity to learn English at a level a good deal higher than "pidgin" English. A worker underground could remain anonymous, but an odd-job man above-ground had to have a name, so that he could be shouted at and called for to do this or do that. It was in this way that when Moses was asked his name and replied "Li Pao-shu," the impatient questioner said, "I'm damned if I can remember that; your name's Moses."

When he got back to China, Moses' brothers took away from him the money he had saved in South Africa, and used it to start a grain-dealing business—the eternal ambition of the peasant, to climb the ladder of social and economic status by becoming a kulak, or employer of other peasants, or still better a dealer in grain and other peasant products. In other words, the peasant reaches out for wealth by exploiting his fellow peasants, within the only part of the social fabric that he knows first hand. I realise now, much too late, how much I could have learned from Moses of the North China peasantry and the grim struggle, more often unsuccessful than successful, to climb out of the peasantry. There would have been no need to "interview" him, using the techniques of the dessicated tribe of sociologists. He loved to talk, and we had many long hours alone in our travels; but alas, I was usually absorbed in writing up my field-notes on something else.

Penniless, and with no help from a bankrupt family, Moses drifted from one job to another, as Eleanor describes. His most realizable asset was his knowledge of English, and with this he at last got a job for several years as "Number One Boy" (in the colonial terminology of the China Coast) in the household of a South African engineer working for the famous Kailan Coal Mines. When the South Africans left China, Moses heard by the grapevine that my parents were looking for a Number One Boy. My father knew Chinese very well, but when Moses applied for the job and was asked his name, he replied "Moses," instead of Li Pao-shu, and so Moses he remained. When my parents left China, he and I inherited each other. We got on beautifully for about five years. Then, when I told him I was going to get married, he was worried. New wives, he said, were bad news for old servants, but in spite of his worries Eleanor soon won him over, and whenever I made an important decision he was not satisfied until I told him Eleanor had approved.

There is a story about Moses that shows a bit of Eleanor's quality as well as telling something about Moses and something important about China's ancient culture. In 1929 we were in Manchuria—I should get into the habit of calling it the Northeast, because neither the

Introduction to the 1975 Edition

Chinese nor the Manchus themselves ever called it "Manchuria." On one occasion I left Eleanor and Moses in Mukden, while I went off alone into the Western, Mongol-inhabited part of the province. We were then not at all sure of our future, nor how long we were going to be able to stay in China. Eleanor was worried about what would happen to Moses. Obviously, he could best earn money by working for a foreign family, but he was quite illiterate in Chinese, let alone English. Eleanor's idea was that he could get a much better job if he could learn to write a little English, even if only enough to keep simple marketing accounts.

Moses learned the alphabet in a couple of days. He could read A, B, C, when you showed them to him, and write them when you said to him, "Write A, write B, write C." Then Eleanor started on syllables, AR, CAR, and so on. This went slowly, so Eleanor went on to whole words, thinking that perhaps a whole word, with a meaning to it, would be easier to memorize, and that the learning of whole words would gradually instill the principle of combining letters into syllables. So at the beginning of the next lesson she wrote out CARROT and showed it to Moses. He looked at at blankly.

"Come on," said Eleanor, "it's not hard. What are the letters?"

"C-A-R-R-O-T," said Moses, reading them off without hesitation.

Introduction to the 1975 Edition

"That's fine," said Eleanor. "Exactly right. Now what's the word?"

Moses looked at it for a long time, with the expression, or lack of expression, that Eleanor used to call "poker-faced." Then, like a gambler making a desperate throw, he said firmly: "Potatoes."

I am not telling this story to make fun of Moses, but because it helps to explain—and it would take a long and learned study to explain it as well—something of major importance in the history of civilization in China, namely, the Chinese system of writing. From the earliest times Chinese writing has been extremely complicated. It contains hints and suggestions of both sound and meaning (which were originally pictures or diagrams), but nothing remotely resembling an alphabet. To be able to read and write requires a massive exercise of memory, and this is true even today, in spite of the great and intelligent efforts of the present government to increase and rationalize education. In the past, the society of China included a small literate elite and a huge mass of illiterates—and there is no doubt that the elite preferred things that way; it kept them in power. One consequence was that peasants and people of peasant origin, like Moses, were convinced to the marrow of their bones of two things about writing: that it meant money and power, and that it was not rational. It meant memorizing an immense repertory of hints and suggestions which were never clear statements of either sound or meaning. In a culture in which the writing is alphabetic, an illiterate may know some letters, but be unable to read them when grouped together as words. In China—the old China—the illiterate frequently could recognize some whole words (the "characters"), but had no rational system for breaking them down into their component parts—the "brush-strokes" of the "characters." Moses, a man of common sense in practical affairs, assimilated the idea of an alphabet to the nature of the Chinese writing: it was a mass of squiggles, and perhaps if he memorized letters not as statements of sound, but as hints and suggestions, he would from the general shape of the word be able to memorize its pronunciation and meaning.

After Manchuria in 1929–30 we came to Peking and lived there until the end of 1937, when the tightening Japanese hold on North China made it impossible for me to continue the kind of work I was doing. Our life was idyllic, with Moses presiding over the household. Our son was born there in 1931, and by the time we left Peking in 1937 he spoke more Chinese than English. Caring for the small child limited Eleanor's travelling, but I took up the study of Mongol and travelled frequently in Inner Mongolia, though I made no more long journeys. Our house became a center for Mongols visiting Peking.

Introduction to the 1975 Edition

Then came the years in America, from 1938 to 1963. Eleanor, who could easily have become a professional architect, planned and supervised the building of a lovely house on a wooded hillside, filled with the lovely things we had brought from China. And then the happy years in England, from 1963 to 1970. We lived successively in two houses, each made beautiful by Eleanor's genius for knowing both what to do to a house and how to live in it.

In 1961 and 1969 we made long visits to Mongolia, where we made a number of close, warm friendships, and in England our house became once more a center for Mongols, because of the students coming from Mongolia to the University of Leeds.

Those English years brought us another echo of Mongolia, and an extraordinary echo of Eleanor's "Turkestan Reunion." In 1943, at the height of Japan's imperialist expansion, a young Japanese woman, newly married, was preparing to accompany her husband to Inner Mongolia. Both young people were against Japan's imperialism, but neither belonged to the organised or the underground left. They wanted to find something to do that would be of the least possible help to their country's mad imperialist adventure. (How pathetically that anticipated the scruples of so many American university intellectuals who have since tried to keep out of the way of American imperialism!) The husband was trained in a combination of law and sociology, so the way out was an assignment to study the remnants of "tribal" or "customary" law in Inner Mongolia. The wife went along because they were young and modern and did not believe in the old feudal custom of the husband's going abroad while the wife sat patiently at home.

Her training had been in English language and literature. (Her first publication was a translation of Louisa May Alcott's *Little Women.*) Looking for something to prepare her for the unknowns of life in Inner Mongolia, she found a pirated Japanese translation of *Turkestan Reunion*. It wasn't Mongolia, but it was Central Asia, and it was by a woman. it enthralled her.

The next year, 1944, the young couple made a difficult winter journey, in camel carts, to Ujumchin, then one of the most remote regions of Inner Mongolia, little touched by the outside influences, and clinging to traditional Mongol ways of life. It was terribly cold, and part of the time they did not even have a tent, but slept on the open steppe. The young Japanese wife was determined not to give up. To prepare herself, she read Eleanor's book again. "If that American woman could do it," she said, "I can do it"—and she stuck it out.

Twenty years later, in our first year in England I got a letter from her. In the years after the war she had been active in the Japanese branch of the Women's International League for Peace and Freedom (founded by Jane

Addams), and because of her excellent knowledge of English and French was frequently sent to Europe. She came to see me at the University, and later came to stay with Eleanor and me. Her interest in Mongolian studies was revived, and that was how Fujiko Isono came into our lives. Later she and her husband, Professor Seiichi Isono, spent an academic year at Leeds, he studying principally English "family courts" and she working under my supervision in Mongolian studies. Later, she spent another year at Leeds as a Visiting Lecturer, and also made two independent visits to the Mongolian People's Republic. She now continues to work in collaboration with me in Mongolian studies, but her talents are so great that she will make her own independent, permanent place in the world of scholarship.

In 1970 I retired from my university chair at Leeds, and we came to America to start the building of a new house, in Virginia. As the plane was landing in New York, Eleanor suffered a massive stroke. It was a crowning mercy. She never knew what happened. No pain, no fear, no premonition. But that was the end of what one of her friends called "a honeymoon of forty-four years." Readers of this book will understand how Eleanor's genius for love and friendship, and her zest for life, made the whole of our life together a honeymoon.

Owen Lattimore

INTRODUCTION

T HESE letters were written on my
wedding journey when, for a carefree and adventurous
year, Moses and my husband and I wandered over some
of the least known portions of the world. (I put Moses
first because while he was our servant he was really the
most important member of the expedition.)

After meeting, with much difficulty, at Chuguchak on
the Siberian-Turkestan border, we journeyed for long
lovely months with ponies, carts, and camels along the
great North Road and the long South Road of Chinese
Turkestan, the North Road being north and the South
Road being south of the T'ien Shan, or Heavenly Mountains. Our way led us through deserts, mountains, and
oases and at last over the five high passes to Leh and
across the last ridges of the Himalayas to Kashmir, from
which lovely but tourist-ridden land we reëntered the
world, rebelliously.

For a wedding journey Chinese Turkestan seemed to
us, and still seems, a most desirable land, for it is far
away from our familiar world not only in space but in

time. It is cut off from the world on the east by the great Gobi Desert, on the south by the fearsome barrier of the Kuen Lun, Karakorum and Himalayan ranges, and on the north and west by the steppes and deserts and mountains of Siberia and Russian Turkestan. At the time we were there no railway came within a week or ten days of its borders, and its inaccessibility was augmented by the strict isolation policy of its governor, who feared that contact with the outside world would involve him in wars and discord. He, therefore, reigned in mediæval grandeur and squalor over a land uncontaminated by modern life.

In the whole province there was not a bank, and no printing press, except for a small one which printed their new paper money. There were three motor cars, only one of which worked even a little, an ancient Packard, for which there was no gasoline. No newspapers from the outside world were allowed to infect the inhabitants with ideas of progress.

A handful of white men lived in this land as large as France, Germany and Spain put together: one British consul, four Russian consuls, an Irish postal commissioner, four Catholic priests, a few Swedish and English missionaries, some traders, no Americans at all. Travelers, also, have been very few, so it is still a land in the happy state of being very little known.

Anyone can see that it was a lovely place for a wedding journey. Our friends, however, were a little startled when we told them that we expected to spend the first six months of our married life apart. This was because we were in Peking and Chinese Turkestan was a long way off. And we cold bloodedly decided to travel there by different ways. My husband wanted to cross Mongolia by an unexplored and unknown route, traveling with trading caravans which had been forced to its use because the easier and better known routes had been closed by Chinese civil wars and Mongol rebellion. It was for the most part a journey across blank and utter desert. The caravan men scarcely knew the way themselves, and to go with them my husband must travel as a camel man, plodding with the slow camels across yellow sands and black gravel for 1,600 miles, a journey of four months on end. When they got to Turkestan they were not sure that they would be admitted but might have to turn around and plod the four months back again. It all seemed impossible for a woman. And so we planned that if he got into Turkestan he would send back word to me and that I would come around on the Trans-Siberian Railway and down on a little branch line toward the Turkestan border, where he would meet me. That sounded simple enough, but proved in the end to be quite as difficult as the desert journey.

There are bound to be hitches in any project as ambitious as traveling half across Asia. Our first hitch was a

Introduction

Chinese civil war, which commandeered my husband's camels and stopped the trains and marooned us in a mud town on the edge of Mongolia for half a year. So that it turned out to be the second instead of the first six months that we spent apart.

I had come up to Kueihua from Peking to wave good-by to my husband's camel caravan, but it proved to be farewell and hail, for he came back the same day, his camels and everyone else's camels commandeered by the soldiers for the wars. I had brought clothes for a week and stayed six months. They were ragged, happy, exciting months of camping in the hills, playing hide and seek with bandits and never knowing when the retreating soldiers might shoot and loot our town or if we were ever going to get away. But the day finally came when my husband escaped to a caravan hiding in the hills and three weeks later I took the first train out of Kueihua for a hazardous five-day journey back to Peking.

Two months of grimy packets of letters brought to me by caravans my husband had passed on the desert, four months of silence, and then at last a wireless message came instructing me to meet him at Semipalatinsk, and early in February, 1927, I set out happily but rather nervously alone.

Our travels fall naturally into three parts. Our journeys alone—my husband's through Mongolia, and mine through Siberia—were the most difficult; traveling together through Turkestan was the most pleasant; and crossing the high passes to India the most exciting. The first stage I have described in "By Sledge to the Middle Ages" in *The Atlantic Monthly* for January and February, 1928, and my husband in his book, *The Desert Road to Turkestan*. My husband has also written a substantial book, *High Tartary*, about our year in Turkestan.

I could not have made the journey at all without my husband. If I had not believed him to be at the end of the rainbow I could never have traveled alone those seventeen days by sledge across the snow-covered Steppes of the Great Horde in the dead of winter. And later, if I had not been with him I could not have camped with the nomad Kazaks of the Heavenly Mountains, nor kept house in Turkestan deserts and oases, nor finally crossed the five great mountain passes, all over 16,000 feet high, which form the mountain barrier between Turkestan and India. But men go everywhere, and write about it, whereas, as a woman in a land where white women have seldom, and in many places, never been seen, my interests, experiences and sensations were in many ways unique. I am therefore venturing to suppose that there are those who will be interested in my side of our "sentimental journey."

Turkestan Reunion

CHAPTER I. *Of how I set out to meet my husband, of the Trans-Siberian and another railway, of how I didn't find him in Semipalatinsk but did find the Kosloffs, and of how I started with Kitaiski and fourteen loads of matches on a seventeen-day sledge journey through the snow.*

Dearest Family,

YOU know I always did maintain, against the popular assumption and your grave doubts, that a woman could travel alone more easily than a man. A man is expected to look after himself and do things for himself, and besides he is often darkly suspected of being a spy or some sort of subterranean agent, and is in consequence cross-questioned and harried, examined and watched, until he begins to wonder himself if he has any right to be there. Whereas a woman alone, whether she wants it so or not, seems always to be an object of public concern and beneficence. In fact it seems probable that she could travel to any iniquitous city or barbarous country in the world and be convinced that it was full of kindly people. For everywhere there are some who take pleasure in good deeds and she is their involuntary target. To officials she can completely explain her "profession" by the innocuous term of "housewife," and the "purpose of her journey," "to join her husband." These anyone can

3

understand and warm to. Her existence is explained, her journey justified.

And now I feel as if this journey of mine were going to prove or disprove my theory forever, for I am sure that nothing could be much more difficult for a woman to do alone than to set out across the snow wastes of Siberia in the dead of winter toward a vague spot in Central Asia with the ridiculous name of Chuguchak.

Do you remember how, less than three years ago, when Dorothy and I crossed Siberia on a comfortable modern express train, it seemed an adventuresome and daring journey fraught with unknown dangers? How ridiculously simple that seems now compared with what I am about to do! We would walk up and down the platform at stations like the one where I am now and feel delicious thrills at being in Siberia, and yet we felt so protected, knowing that we should jump back onto the train again and shouldn't have to leave it until we were safe in China. I should no more have thought of stopping in a town like this than I should of letting go Mother's hand and venturing across the nursery before I had learned to walk. Yet this morning I watched the Trans-Siberian express disappear into the snowy distance with a feeling of exaltation that now I was really in Siberia with a journey ahead of me into a region few foreigners have traveled.

I have been in Siberia, as a matter of fact, for four

days now, but always under the protection of the friendly express train. So far my journey has been beautifully simple and proved my theory to perfection, for it might easily have been difficult if the world weren't so full of those people who like to be nice to women traveling alone.

In fact I feel as if I had been handed along from place to place on a series of silver platters. In Peking, in the short week I had after Owen's wireless came from Urumchi, everyone set to work helping me, and with shoppings and packings and farewells I left there in a whirl. Then at Mukden a young Englishman, friend of a friend in Peking, tended to all the irksome business of transferring luggage for me, securing my reservation and seeing me safe onto my next train.

The train this time was on the Japanese line which runs from Mukden to Changchun, and had Pullman cars so exactly like those in America that it made me homesick, since I felt already out of China and yet not in America, for the porters were small and Japanese instead of big and black, and there were neatly folded kimonos and leather slippers supplied to destroy the illusion of the curtained berths.

From Changchun to Harbin I felt farther still from China, for the train and porters were Russian. The porters in the Harbin station were Russian, too, and wore big white aprons.

At Harbin I was looked after again by friends of

friends, who helped me to secure my visa for Chinese Turkestan and changed my money, partly into yen for my railway ticket, partly into Harbin dollars for last odds and ends of shopping, and partly into rubles to use in Siberia; who entertained me delightfully and gave me introductions to people in Manchuli and here; and who saw me off at the station with fudge and fruit cake and mince pies.

I wish I could tell you about Harbin, as I am sure it is like no place else on earth. It is a Russian city in China, ugly and crass like other frontier towns, full of riffraff, and famed for the extravagance of its night life and its cabarets crowded with the débris of the Russian imperialist refugees and with Chinese a little carried away by the feeling of race superiority given by their ability to domineer over the rag tag and bobtail of White Russians who form a large part of the city's population. The Chinese flaunt their Russian women in an attempt to live up to the youngsters of the American and European business communities, who flaunt their Russian women in an attempt to live up to the East.

In Manchuli on the Russian border I had to wait a day to arrange with the customs for permission to carry four cameras and a lot of films and photographic supplies through Siberia. I was met at the station by the Chinese postmaster and by Manchuli's only English-speaking inhabitant, the latter a most surprising person to find in that scraggly frontier town—a delightful hermit who raises goldfish and Angora cats and who entertained me charmingly in his little study lined with books and Persian rugs. All my meals in Manchuli I had with him and wished there might be more.

At Manchuli, too, I had my first experience of a Russian hotel, cold and ugly enough, where I managed to ask for tea and hot water, and where a price list on the door, which I laboriously spelled out with the help of my pocket dictionary, informed me how much I must pay for each, as well as for the towel and sheets and pillowcase which I had also ordered in my best phrase-book Russian, and how much I should have had to pay had I had a samovar or a bath.

While I was being entertained by the friendly postmaster or the charming Englishman, by some mysterious means permission was obtained for all my luggage to go through uninspected and my ticket was bought, and I had only to wait in the station master's inner office while other passengers' suitcases were being emptied and their most private belongings exhibited to the public gaze. Then post-office coolies carried my luggage onto the train, where I discovered to my delight that I had a pleasant compartment entirely to myself.

On Russian trains one travels "hard" or "soft" or "wagon-lits"—a "hard" ticket entitling one to an unupholstered berth in a car much like a third-class sleeping car on the Continent, a "soft" ticket to a berth in a well-fitted second-class compartment, and "wagon-lits" to a place on one of the old international sleeping cars taken over by the Trans-Siberian and run only on the semi-weekly express trains. I traveled "soft" and found it clean and comfortable, probably more comfortable with my compartment all to myself than if I'd traveled grandly "wagon-lits," though I was amused to discover that I was looked down on socially by the other foreigners on the train, who spoke of it condescendingly as traveling "Russian" in contrast to traveling "international."

Out of the window of my compartment was snow—crisp, sunny snow everywhere as far as I could see. Lake Baikal was buried deep, with little sleighs darting across it like black flies, and I wondered if they were anything like the sleigh that I should travel in after I left the railway.

It was a great lark to hop out at little stations in the tingling cold and eat a bowl of hot cabbage soup with sour cream in it at the station buffet, or buy a circle of hot fresh bread, new butter, and a little roasted chicken for my supper from a peasant woman at a wooden stall.

After four sunny, snowy days of Siberia I reached here this morning and wished again that I weren't trying to carry quite so much luggage to the middle of Asia. Watching it on and off trains had become a dizzier process at every stop. Here it was speedily loaded on a sledge,

8

and when I told the white-aproned porter I was waiting for the train to Semipalatinsk he trundled it half a block to a sort of left-luggage office and deposited it in a heap on the floor.

I had rather expected I should have to spend this eighteen hours' wait between trains sitting on it in the station, but I find that it would not have been allowed in the station at all, which is far too crowded with people to leave room for their luggage, so I am free of it till 3:45 in the morning, which is the ungodly time my train departs for Semipalatinsk.

The ticket office is closed till train time, and with my six phrases of the Russian language, the jam of passengers, and my jam of luggage I felt quite hopeless about ever getting it and me onto the train without assistance. I had a letter to somebody somewhere here, but when I looked out of the station door the city seemed a long way off and the day felt very cold. However, I took a deep breath and set out.

There was a row of droshkies across from the station. I chose the kindest-looking of the drivers and showed him the address on my letter. He answered with a torrent of language which I finally assorted into meaning that it would cost me five rubles to get there in a droshky, but I could go in an automobile for thirty kopecks.

"Where is the automobile?" I asked.

"I'll show you," volunteered a small boy at my heels,

and led me to the top of the hill, where a motor bus was rapidly filling with passengers.

After a ride of twenty minutes all the passengers helpfully put me off at a street corner, and one of them, who was also dismounting, led me to a building the address of which corresponded to the one on my letter. A great many people lived in the building, none of whom seemed ever to have heard of the man I was looking for until one told me he had moved away, he didn't know where. Well, Novo Sibirsk is a rather large city, and I was on a wide street of shops and public buildings; but, now that it seemed to be difficult, I wanted more than ever to find my friend of the letter. So I kept on showing people the name on the envelope and rather enjoyed the sensation of feeling like a waif. And after a while I was somehow shoved along to a large new office building and into a room filled with clerks and typists and up to a very busy and important-looking man at a desk in one corner. He was friendly and to the point.

"What do you want?" he asked.

"I want someone to buy my ticket and help me onto the train for Semipalatinsk tonight," I answered.

"Very well," he said, and spoke to a clerk.

In a minute a villainous-looking chap in a huge fur hat swaggered in. He looked like a very tough driver of a very big brewery wagon.

"This man," said my friend, "will do all you want. He

10

will come to the station at ten tonight. Pay him three rubles for his services. Is there anything else?"

"No, thank you," I answered gratefully, and came back to the station.

I am ensconced here in the first-class buffet, a small room with a fancy counter covered with fruit in piles and pastries in rows, and two long tables covered with once white cloths and laden with rubber plants and Christmas trees in pots and silver candelabra and three-tiered cake plates, and surrounded by a varied collection of jaded travelers, all of the men in high boots and huge coats of every known kind of fur and fur hats, some of them quite as big as dishpans. And all of them have beards. Siberia should have been called "Sibeardia!"

In the waiting room outside, too, there is a wonderful collection of humans—Buriats and Tatars and Mongols and others of the strange races who occupy corners of Siberia, many of them, in fur hats and tight-waisted coats and high boots, looking exactly like various versions of Santa Claus.

My guide may look like a ruffian, but he seems to have a good heart. He has just come in, though it is only three instead of ten, and has gallantly brought me some tea and cakes and settled down to be friendly. With the aid of my pocket dictionary we have been holding spirited conversation. He has no feeling for the alphabet at all, but is indefatigable in thumbing through pages of the dictionary until he finds the word he wants. He has told me how many Communists there are in England, in France, in Germany, and the total for the world, and has asked me numberless questions about both China and America. I am writing this while he looks up words in order to tell me something new and remarkable about Soviet Russia. "Did you know John Reed?" he has just asked me. "I worship him. He was Russia's wonderful friend."

He has also been pointing out to me various individuals here in the waiting room and whispering to me darkly that they are "White" and "no true friends of Russia." Then, pointing to a young woman across the table with whom I had been trying to talk before he came in, he scrambled through the dictionary to point out to me that she was an "entertainer of suspected persons."

This city used to be called Novo Nikolayevsk until the people who no longer honor Czars changed it to "New Siberia," and it has been growing fast since the building of the branch railway to Semipalatinsk has brought Central Asian commerce here instead of by river to Omsk. And it is a New Siberia. I wish I could tell you what a feeling I have had of the difference between the people here and on the train and the Russians of the old Russia whom I have known in New York and Peking. The latter live so tragically in the past, whereas these people live so hopefully for the future.

Turkestan Reunion

But my ardent guide has brought me some soup, so I must change my pencil for a spoon. I'll write more on the train.

February 2

I am on the last train I'll see this year, and not only is it a very strange train, but I am very surprised to be here.

At ten last night my guide was still entertaining me when a woman with a shawl over her head came up and muttered in his ear. "That's my wife," he grinned. "She wants me to come home. I'll be back before one to tend to your luggage."

As my train didn't leave till 3:45 I hadn't worried when at one he hadn't returned. But a few minutes after one the "entertainer of suspected persons" came rushing up to me, talking very excitedly, and others joined her, all trying to explain something to me in very rapid Russian, which I finally gathered to be that there was a rule that no baggage would be weighed and checked after one o'clock, also that the left-luggage room closed at one. Well, I knew that a rule was a rule in Russia. I'd been running into them all day. No luggage allowed in the waiting room. No sleeping allowed in the station. It was almost as bad as America. I began to see visions of waiting another twenty-four hours in the station without sleeping, and knew it couldn't be done.

By this time a crowd had collected, all trying to tell me what to do. But the young woman took me by the arm and marched me to the baggage room, where the man was just locking up. He was surly at first, but weakened at her tale of my sad plight and promised to wait till I could bring my stuff to be weighed. Then we rushed to the left-luggage office half a block away and found it locked. She banged on the door and a very cross man appeared, but she finally melted him too and he promised to keep open till we could find a porter.

But we couldn't find a porter. She told my tale to every porter in the station, but they were all busy. Finally we went to the first baggage man with a second tale of woe. He was grumpy, but produced a porter, and the porter got my eleven pieces of baggage over in several trips, my efficient friend waiting at one baggage room and I at the other; it was weighed, I paid the excess, and we sat on it till train time, having kept both baggage offices open an hour after their closing time.

All this to prove that it is lucky for women traveling alone that there are so many Boy-Scout-intentioned people in the world.

Miss Entertainer of Suspected Persons was very friendly and saw me onto the train, which was a good thing, too, as the porter put me on the wrong car and there was a most awful fuss and I shouldn't have known what it was all about.

Just before the train started, who should appear but the faithless guide, with a pathetic tale of how he had gone to sleep, and demanding his three rubles for what he hadn't done; and since I couldn't explain to a car of interested spectators about how he hadn't earned it, it seemed easier to pay.

This train is all "hard," but I slept well on my broad berth, across from a frowzy woman in a red kerchief who ate raw fish in the middle of the night. We are jogging slowly across more fields of snow, stopping longer than we go and yet running quite according to schedule. This leisurely rate gives me long walks at the tiny stations, where I buy *piroshkies,* delicious hot meat pastries, and eat them as I walk and feel farther and farther away from anything I have ever known before.

Tomorrow I reach Semipalatinsk, the jumping off place where we start our long trip by sleigh to Chinese Turkestan. I say "we" because Owen's wireless message said that he would meet me at the end of the railway. However, with all the difficulties of winter travel and of crossing the Russian frontier I don't dare count on his really being there.

Turkestan Reunion

Life becomes more and more surprising. You'd be aghast at where I am living, but it's wonderful—a tenement room with a family of four and a dog and a cat and two boarders. And none of them can speak anything that I can speak, but just the same we have a merry time.

This journey is being so difficult that I feel more exhilarated and on top of the world each time I accomplish a stage of it. Whereas certainly the fact that I am here at all is no credit to me, but only because Russia is so full of nice people.

I must confess that when I reached here I felt somewhat as if I had come to a blank wall across my way, and that a rendezvous with one's husband at Semipalatinsk *or* Chuguchak seemed almost as impossible as everyone in Peking had told us it was. For Owen wasn't here, and I discovered that in spite of my firm resolution I *had* counted quite a lot on finding him waiting on the snowy station platform when I tumbled wearily out of the train at the end of the line. But when I arrived, after thirty-three hours "hard," and climbed out of the dim car into a glittering world of snow, there wasn't any husband, but only a forlorn wooden railway station in the midst of a vast white plain, far across which I could see the roofs and onion-shaped church towers of the city.

The other passengers all seemed to know where they were going. They flocked from the train straight into funny little sleighs and jingled briskly off across the plain. Only the frowzy woman paid any attention to me. Her husband had met her and they watched my luggage in the car while the porter made trips back and forth. Then they, too, slid off in a tiny raft of a sleigh lined with straw, and I was left alone on an empty platform wondering what to do next.

I wasn't alone long, for I was soon assaulted by a mob of drivers all inviting me with howls to ride in their sleighs. They were mostly grinning red-skinned Orientals, Sarts or Tatars, and they had comic little sleighs about the size and shape of baby carriages attached to horses that looked huge and raw-boned compared with China ponies.

My only move was to find a woman about whom I knew nothing at all except that her name was Kosloff and that her husband worked in the post office. I had met her brother when we were marooned in Kueihua last summer and he had given me a letter to her. So I picked the least ruffian-looking driver; he piled his baby carriage with my luggage, and me perched on top, till I was certain we'd topple over. And sure enough we did, right in the middle of the plain. The sleigh turned quite over, the driver and I and the luggage flew in all directions, and the horse ran away.

Everything retrieved, we drove into the city, across a great market-place full of Russians and strange Orientals and stalls and carts of produce, past a wild-looking chap galloping in with a string of huge horses, the halter of each tied to the tail of the one in front, and to the post office, where I found Kosloff. He was cordial and sent me on home to his wife.

We drove up to a two-story unpainted log house and I banged on the front door to no effect. I went around to the back and a woman in a shawl pointed me up some steep stairs and through a door into a kitchen littered with dirty dishes, remnants of food, dogs, cats, and babies, where several women with rough red hands and faces were working. A merry roly-poly girl owned to being Mrs. Kosloff and took me into her little room, a typical tenement-house room where she and her husband, two small children, the dog and the cat, all lived together in grubby squalor.

The Kosloffs insisted on my staying with them, which seemed impossible, as, except for sharing a kitchen with the other occupants of the tenement, they had only the one room, which was nearly half filled with my luggage. But I saw they were going to be really offended if I would not accept their hospitality, so here I am. Mr. Kosloff has given me his bed, two boards on horses, Chinese style, and he sleeps on the floor.

Mr. Kosloff came home at four and we had dinner— a *piroque,* which was a sort of fish pie, soup, and little birds. We sat on packing boxes around an oilcloth-covered table. There weren't enough dishes and everything was dirty, but it tasted wonderful, as it was my first real meal since leaving Manchuli a week ago. Mrs. Kosloff feeds two men who live in the next room, as well as her own family.

It is easy to see that the Kosloffs have not always lived as they do now, and I liked their manner of being apologetic about and at the same time unashamed of their poverty. We have had great fun laughing over our pocket-dictionary conversations, and they have told me a little about themselves. At the time of the Revolution many of their friends and relatives fled from Russia and some took an active part in General Anenkoff's attacks against the Bolsheviks from across the Turkestan border. They themselves were undecided whether to attempt to flee to America or remain in Russia, but could not bear the idea of living in any other country and so stayed on, hoping for the gradual return of prosperity under Communist rule. The Communists, however, were suspicious of them because of their many connections with imperialists. For a while Mr. Kosloff was imprisoned and later had much difficulty obtaining work, and, while he has become a thoroughly loyal Communist, it is only very recently that he has been really trusted by his party.

They seem very confident that better times are coming soon, and suffer their poverty cheerfully for what they consider a great cause. The two handsome youths who board with them, now actors in a local company, also talked of Communism ardently and with the idealism of youth, and the little girl proudly showed me pictures of Lenin in her school book.

February 4

I slept well on my board bed, and helped wash last night's greasy dishes in a saucer of water with no soap and dried them with a dirty rag. Then we had breakfast of the cold remains of the fish pie, tea, and bread and butter. The room was cold, shivery cold, and the baby spread his tea over most of the table and hit us all with his spoon. They feed him all the sugar he yells for. Neither the dog, the cat, nor the baby is housebroken.

After breakfast we made a gesture of cleaning up and Mrs. Kosloff took me to the Soviet House to register. It was bitter cold, but sunny. It all looked exactly as a Siberian town should look—houses of plaster or logs, lining wide snowy streets that lead to a green-domed church. On the way home we stopped in the market to

buy fresh butter and honey and black bread. Everywhere
I have been in Siberia food seems plentiful and very
cheap, though other prices are high. It was there in the
market-place, with its frontier mixture of races and cos-
tumes and its camels and horses and ponies, that I realized that I was really at the gateway of Central Asia.

But what really worries me is that I can't get in touch
with Owen and so have no way of knowing where he is.
I hoped at least to find letters or a telegram here, but
none have come. There is a telegraph line from here to
the Turkestan border, from which messages can be sent
by courier to the Russian consul in Chuguchak to be de-
livered if advisable. I sent two messages but no answer has
reached me.

I can only assume that he has been held up at Chuguchak and not allowed to cross the Russian frontier. I
have known all along that there was a possibility of this,
because between the time when Owen sent his wireless
message from Urumchi, saying that he could meet me
here and the time I left Peking our government, as you've
probably seen in the papers, refused to allow the Soviet
ambassadress to Mexico to travel through United States
territory on her way to her new post, and as a consequence the Soviet government is automatically refusing
visas to all Americans wishing to enter Russia. I had
friends in Peking who were able to secure mine in spite

of the new rule but Owen would not have the same help in Chuguchak.

The other possibility is that he is on the way from Chuguchak here and has been held up on the road. From what we hear of the condition of the road this also is not unlikely. However, I was told at the Soviet House that I must leave Semipalatinsk in two days in order to cross the border before my visa expires, so I can't wait here much longer on the chance that he will come. But it would be tragic to pass him on the way. It is all very confusing.

I am certainly not going to spoil the trip by turning around and going home, and since I can't stay here I suppose I will have to get to Chuguchak some way or other. It must be possible. Chuguchak is on the map, and other people go there. But it is four hundred miles away, across desolate wastes of snow. The road, they tell me, is well-nigh impossible and the cold terrific. To get there I must hire a sleigh and, if possible, I must find a traveling companion, as the sleigh drivers are unreliable and there are Kirghiz bandits on the road. And I'm sure I don't know how to accomplish all this. The people here seem horrified at the idea of my attempting it. Of course, lack of language is my chief difficulty, as my Russian is quite inadequate for anything so complicated.

Mrs. Kosloff enterprisingly accosted every group of Orientals we met while we were out to ask if they had come from Chuguchak and how they came and what the road was like. They all reported that the road is bad and cold and that it takes from ten to twenty days to make the trip. We've followed several clues as to possible drivers, all in vain, and now I feel balked and discouraged and at a loss what to do next.

February 6

Suddenly I seem to be on my way.

Instead of living in the Kosloff's merry, grubby tenement I am sitting on the felt-covered floor of a mud-walled, low-ceilinged Kazak hut, with scarcely enough light to write by at nine o'clock in the morning, for the hut is buried in snow.

But first I must tell you how I got here. Yesterday morning, still no telegram, and only one day left. My Russian friends had failed to find a sleigh for me, so I determined to look for one myself. I went first to the Chinese consulate, thinking that they must have made arrangements there for Chinese travelers passing through and might be able to help me. The consul was cordial, and I was so stirred to find someone with whom I could talk that my Chinese has never been so fluent.

He told me that a courier from the consulate was starting out that very afternoon, traveling down with some cargo, and that I could go with him if I wished. I shied a little when I heard "cargo," knowing how slowly freight usually travels, but he assured me that we shouldn't be more than ten days on the road. He spoke of it as a wonderful opportunity, and yet when it came I was almost afraid to take it because I hadn't heard from Owen. I explained my fears to him and he reassured me again, saying that even if he had started from Chuguchak I couldn't miss him, as there was only one road and everyone traveling it stopped at the same inns at night. So he called the courier, a merry Chinese youth, and it was all arranged on the spot that a sleigh would call for me at three that afternoon.

It was then twelve. Mrs. Kosloff dumped the baby with a neighbor and went out to help me buy food for the trip and big felt boots. Everyone in Siberia wears felt boots to the knees, huge and shapeless and awkward to walk in, but the only things to keep feet warm in this bitter climate. I tried on a dozen pairs in as many little stalls in the market before I found some that were in the least comfortable.

The sleigh was waiting when we got home, and Mr. Kosloff with a bottle of vodka, which he said I must drink when I got cold but must not give to the drivers. I packed and got into my fur-lined leather suit in a great rush and swallowed some dinner and kissed all the Kosloffs. They had been so generous and hospitable that I wished I could have done more for them than leave some clothes behind that I said I hadn't room for.

We drove to the inn from which we were to start and found fourteen sledges in the yard all loaded with crates of matches. It seemed that the courier and I were supposed to perch on top of the matches. The consul had told me that the courier was taking two sleighs and that I should have one all to myself, but the courier assured me that fourteen sledges were better than two because of bandits, and he had the drivers arrange one of them more comfortably for me.

The sledges are crude triangular little rafts made of a rough network of small logs and dragged along on very low runners. The usual passenger sleighs have covers over them, something like a Peking cart, and are pulled by two horses, but these were quite uncovered, and as they were heavily loaded and had only one horse apiece my heart sank to think how slowly they would travel.

The Russian drivers, who look like pirates but seem to be good-hearted enough, fixed a little nest for me, put straw on the logs and my bed roll on top of that, and matches and my luggage all around the edge. There isn't room to stretch out my legs, so I get cramped, but it is better than being exposed to the weather.

They were hours getting ready to start, with a great bustle of roping boxes and feeding horses and mending harness. The sun had set and I thought they were really ready at last when everyone yelled *"Chai pit!"* ("Drink tea!") and we all piled into the low, dark little inn. It was full of men sitting around long rough tables, and fitted exactly my picture of what a den of bandits ought to look like. The men were swarthy and unshaven and were dressed in rough, dirty sheepskin clothes with gay sashes around their waists.

A red-bearded chap at the head of one table, evidently the innkeeper, was settling accounts with a crowd of men, which consisted in much shouting and pounding of the table till I thought there'd be a riot. At another table there was a huge samovar and men were drinking tea out of wooden bowls and munching hunks of black bread. They called to me to sit down with them and gave me a bowl of tea and sugar for it. They all seem to know the Chinese courier, and call him *"Kitaiski,"* which means "Chinese."

We were off at last, about seven. The drivers tucked me into my sleeping bag as far as I could get, with my big boots and fur suit and big fur coat on top of that, and covered me over with fur and canvas till I thought I could never get cold, though the town thermometer registered forty degrees below zero Fahrenheit when we left.

I couldn't see out of my nest at all, and we went crunching along on the snow with bells jingling for what seemed like days and nights before we stopped. And when we did I was so numb that I could scarcely struggle out from under cover. When I got my head out the world seemed very weird indeed—nothing but wide stretches of snow in every direction. Misty flurries of snow were falling and there was no light but the light from the snow. The air felt biting cold on my face. In the dim white light I could see that the drivers were unhitching the horses, which seemed mysterious, as there was no sign of any shelter.

Then I saw that they were leading them into a black hole in a snowdrift. Kitaiski went in, too, and I tumbled out of my sledge and followed him. He lit matches so I could see a little. We were in a great low square cave full of horses, on the far side of which was a mud wall and a little door in the wall about three feet high. It all seemed like the weirdest kind of an Arabian Night—out of a completely white and empty world into that black cave of horses, the flare of a match lighting it a little way; the brown side of a great horse, heads of others; then darkness and stumbling till the next flare.

Then the little door pulled open and we climbed into another wide low room, smoke-filled, and lit with candle-light and firelight. Near the door a scrawny woman in a loose, dirty, white cotton garment and a once white kerchief was stuffing great branches of twigs into a crackling fire in a low mud fireplace. Behind her, in the center of the room, was a round table about a foot high with a samovar beside it and pirate drivers sitting around it drinking tea. In dark corners sleepy heads were appearing from under bed covers and brown arms and legs struggling into white clothes.

Kitaiski led me into an inner room, where the floor was covered with felts and a dozen figures were sleeping. I looked at my watch and it was two o'clock. Kitaiski helped me bring in my bed roll and I was soon asleep on the floor.

I was half conscious of a good deal of talking and shouting and opening and closing of doors all night, but the first time I really wakened daylight was beginning to creep in through the one tiny window, where a shaft was dug from the surface of the snow. An old woman crawled out from under covers on a wooden bed against the wall. I watched her dress and wash in a basin of water and go over to the little window, kneel, and bow her head to the ground, muttering prayers all the while, all this in the half dawn. Then children began to cry and other women appeared and dressed them. They brought out a low, round table and a samovar and invited Kitaiski and me to have tea with the family.

I fished a loaf of bread out of the sack in my sledge to eat with my tea, and it was frozen as hard as a lump of ice. The old woman put it on the top of the samovar to thaw.

Kitaiski tells me these people are Kazaks, a tribe of Kirghiz. The Russians call them all Kirghiz, but the true

Kirghiz live mostly south of here. They are Mohammedans, though not very strict about it. He can talk their
queer guttural language. The women wear white kerchiefs with a square of red embroidery under the chin
and loose calico clothes, full, long gowns and tight short-
skirted jackets, and silver rings, bracelets, and earrings.

The only pieces of furniture in the room are two
wooden beds, curved up at the ends like a Chinese sacri-
fice table, but lower and wider. They are painted in gay
colors and piled high with different-colored felts and
quilts that were used by the members of the family,
who slept on the floor.

The outer room, where the drivers slept and had their
tea, is also occupied by cats and puppies and chickens
and tiny lambs in pens. There are saddles and harnesses
and queer crude implements hanging on the walls, and
a fire of twigs is crackling in a little mud stove.

It is very cold outside and the wind is blowing bitterly.
I have always thought of Siberia as a land of exiles, chain
gangs, desert wastes, cold, strange people, and strange
languages, and this really feels like that Siberia.

February 7

Life is gorgeous and wonderful. We're having weather.
Weather always stirs me, and now I am not watching it

through a windowpane. I have been right in it all day, with no roof over my head. All day there has been a snowstorm, a real blizzard, biting wind and whirls of snow, but the horses struggle through it, the drivers shouting and whistling to them and beating them out of holes in the road. The road is scarcely a road at all, but only a long trail which goes up and down like a roller coaster over endless stretches of snow. We bump and bounce along, half the time along the side of hummocks at almost right angles with the earth. Most of the sledges have completely capsized during the day and I expected mine to at any minute with all my luggage on top of me, but I finally learned, as one does in a sailboat, that just at the minute one is sure it will capsize it usually rights itself.

I had to stay under cover most of the time because of the icy wind, so I just jounced along and trusted in the gods.

There was always something the matter with one or another of the sledges, so that we stood still more than we went, and at five o'clock, when we reached another Kazak hut, we had traveled only twenty versts. Kitaiski says there are huts or little mud villages all along the road where we shall stop to rest. They are the only shelter on the way and are from twenty to thirty versts apart, thus dividing the road into what the drivers call *stanka* or stages. Today we have done only one *stanka*, whereas, if we are to reach Chuguchak in ten days, we need to cover two or three a day.

Our lodging tonight is much like last night's except that it is smaller and dirtier. When I went out this morning I saw that we were in a tiny village of huts all buried in the snow, and tonight we are in an exact duplicate. All that is visible are doors in the snowdrifts and chimneys sticking out the top. There are sledges at them all, and it seems quite hopeless to think of finding Owen on the road if he has started.

CHAPTER II. *Of bitter winds and bad roads and life in snow-buried Kazak huts, of how I drove my own sledge through a blizzard, how Kitaiski rescued me from the match caravan and how we arrived six days late to find my bearded husband at a place on the map called Chuguchak.*

DEAREST FAMILY,

IT has stormed for two days and two
nights and I have never been so cold. I stay under cover
all the time for fear of freezing my nose.

Kitaiski has given me a dreadful scare about my nose.
The morning after we started he looked at me with hor-
ror and said excitedly, "Mrs., you have frozen your nose.
The tip of it will certainly fall off." Sure enough, there
was no feeling in it at all. I began rubbing it frantically,
and pretty soon feeling came back, a great deal of feeling. But he is convinced that I shall freeze it on this trip
and says I must carry a mirror with me and keep looking
at it to see if it is white. So I have been nursing it carefully, and the few times I have had the courage to take
a hand out from under cover to fish out the mirror it
has been very red indeed.

At the beginning of every march I climb into my sleeping bag—fur suit, fur coat, big felt boots and all—then
the men tuck me in, put all sorts of things over me, and
pull the canvas over my head. I feel suffocated and can't

move. We ride six or eight hours at a time. After about the fourth hour I get so stiff and cramped that it seems as if I had to move. With a mighty effort I turn a little to one side. This makes a crack somewhere for the cold and I begin slowly to congeal. It starts with my toes and sends little shivers of cold up through my bones, and I get gradually shiverier and stiffer until I wonder which will happen first—that we arrive or I stiffen completely. I move everything that's movable, toes, fingers, and nose, but it doesn't help much.

Last night I tried thinking of other times in my life when I have been as physically uncomfortable—when I was on my back with flu in a little pest-house in the Idaho sagebrush; when I was very seasick on the Empress of Asia; riding all day on a donkey across a scorching Shansi plain; thirty hours on a crowded troop train from Kalgan to Peking. That's about all I could think of.

I lie cold and cramped for hours thinking of people and places and happenings I hadn't thought about for years. And all the while I listen, listen for a sleigh that might be coming past with Owen in it, and then for the barking of dogs, which means the end of the stage and a fire and food and sleep.

Long before we reach a hut we hear the barking, and it cheers me so that I scarcely mind that the dogs are fierce and leap at me when I climb out of my sledge. Then there is the stumbling on numb feet through the stable and fumbling for the little door into the hut. The door is always padded heavily with felt so that it fits tightly into the door frame, and is tugged open and shut with handles of leather thong. When I find the handle in the dark and yank, it opens suddenly to reveal the little smoke-filled room and a frowzy woman starting to build a fire. I find a broom of twigs in a corner to brush the snow from my felt boots before it melts to make them soggy, and step around the lambs and kids and babies to deposit my bed roll in a corner.

There are sudden gusts of cold as the men climb in from the dark after tending to their horses. They throw their boots and sheepskins by the fire and start unwinding their feet. Next to their horses their feet are their chief concern, and each has his pet device for keeping warm. One encases his in camel's wool before putting on his boots, another wraps his in bits of newspaper, and a third in a dreadful assortment of dirty rags. Kitaiski's felt boots turn up at the toes, and last night he cut up his pet fur hat, a sort of Cossack affair with a scarlet top and a swathe of long curly black astrakhan, to make himself additional stockings.

Then, sitting on the felts with a border of gnarled and grimy bare feet about the eight-inch-high table, we drink bowl after bowl of tea and eat hard hunks of bread which one of the men has poured onto the table from a grain sack. One of the Kazak women makes the tea with chips scraped from a hard black brick. She rakes coals from the fire to set the pot on and works steadily to keep our bowls all filled. Whenever one has had enough to eat and drink he flops back where he is on the floor to go to sleep, and soon the room is full of snoring till the driver who is watching outside comes in to call the others loudly and kick them hard till they get up to tend to their horses.

February 10

We reached here at one, after going steadily but, oh, so slowly since seven this morning. The wind has almost died, and all morning the sun struggled to shine through a gray sky. It is the first time I've been able to ride with my head out from under cover and the first time I haven't been cold since we started, and just as we drove into the inn yard the sun really broke through and turned the sky blue. I didn't want to stop at all. It is being a beautiful afternoon, but the drivers had a chance to buy some mutton here and it is not nearly cooked yet, at 4:30, so heaven knows when we shall be on the way again.

This is the end of the sixth day and we have gone about two hundred versts instead of the three hundred and sixty we should have gone. I try not to be impatient, for it is being a gorgeous trip. If I only knew where Owen was and that I was really going toward him I should be hugely enjoying myself.

We passed two covered sleighs today, trotting along at an enviable pace. I called "Owen" at them at the top of my lungs, to the amazement of my driver. It gave me a sinking feeling to watch them drive out of sight and to think he might have been inside. It is almost better to be under cover and not see the sleighs that pass, since there is nothing I can do about it anyway. When we got here I trudged up the snowy street and looked at all the sleighs in all the yards, and when I got back the drivers and Kitaiski were squatting around the low table guzzling tea and munching bread. They are burning branches of cedar in the little stove, which makes the room very fragrant.

The men have been teasing my driver about some escapade of his last night, the fine points of which I miss in spite of Kitaiski's noblest efforts to explain, which explanation, in order to maintain my reputation as a perfect lady, I feign not to understand at all. It seems that in the small hours of the morning he attempted to seduce the young daughter of the Kazak household, offering her five kopecks for her services. Whereupon she got the giggles and squealed loudly, "You can't love *me* for five kopecks. Half a ruble is my price," thereby waking everybody in the house. The poor driver will never hear the end of it. They are already calling him "Five Kopecks."

Turkestan Reunion

The hut we stayed at last night had gorgeously colored felts on the floor and especially gaudy beds and a glowing Russian samovar, but the room was unbearably hot. "House warm, bugs many," remarked Kitaiski. He scratches perpetually, but fortunately I am not yet infested.

An old hag who sat up on top of the stove with a baby demanded to know if I were Kitaiski's wife. "Of course not," said Kitaiski. "Can't you see that she is a foreigner?" "Is she Russian?" the old woman asked. "She's not a Kazak nor a Mongol, so she must be Chinese or Russian. And if you're not married why are you traveling with her?"

Horses are being hitched at last, and we have had our mutton. A great platter of boiled hunks was put in the middle of the low table and the two drivers who own knives cut it into little bits. We carefully waited till they had finished to give them an equal chance with us, then sat around on the floor and set to with our fingers. Unappetizing as it was, it was welcome after six days of frozen bread and bad tea and I ate heartily. We finished by drinking the water it was cooked in, which made a very good soup.

Turkestan Reunion

February 11

One of our horses died this morning. Our sledges were already overloaded, but its load was distributed among them to make them go a little slower. And when we got here at two we found two Chinese men with a two-horse sleigh and no luggage who have already been on the road ten days from Chuguchak.

It is now five and the men are starting to cook more mutton. Last night we rode from seven to one and I got very cold. Tonight it will probably be eight or nine to two or three.

We slept last night in an awful little hole, barely room for us all on the floor, like sardines. Everyone snored and the air got unbearable. The men drank tea till three and were up at five to tend to the horses. We were off at seven, still windy but bright sun, and I tried walking some. Too many clothes to make much progress.

Day after day after day of nothing but snow. I'm having a good dose of the "great open spaces." Today I loved it, jogging endlessly along and being able to look forever and ever into space, never seeing anyone but the driver of my sledge, never saying a word to anyone.

Two or three times a day we pass a string of sledges bringing cotton or skins from Chuguchak. We pass them in silence, and except for them there is complete solitude.

Turkestan Reunion

I was awakened this morning by dogs barking and knew we had arrived at another stopping place. We had ridden all night and I had slept in the sledge. We didn't get started till eleven last night, the reason being that the drivers sent a man back to skin the dead horse. He will get the meat—great feasting in the village—and the drivers paid him two rubles to get the skin for them.

I spent the evening discussing life with Kitaiski. He thinks that China is several times as civilized as Russia, with which he is inclined to class all foreign countries, and makes Turkestan out a veritable paradise. There are no wars, because it is surrounded by deserts and mountains. There are no robbers, because, if a man is caught robbing, the governor immediately executes him, even though he has stolen only a loaf of bread. There are no poor people and everyone has plenty to eat. Even the poorest eat only fine white flour, and every kind of fruit is very cheap. Nor does it get cold as it does in Siberia. In Siberia the people are all thieves and liars and there is no justice. A murderer is punished with only a year or two in jail, and it costs a whole ruble to get a bath.

The drivers and Kitaiski are very nice to me. They are crude, of course, and have a lot of vulgar jokes at my expense, but they don't know that I understand them at all and are always polite and respectful to me. They tease Kitaiski about me, but he takes it good-naturedly.

A little brown lamb has just jumped off the bed onto my lap. The old hag here is spinning wool onto a twirling stick. Her daughter has a four-day-old baby that bleats like the little lamb when it cries. She has rigged up a little cradle for it dug out of a log of wood. She herself works around the house as if nothing had happened to her, building fires and waiting on the drivers.

There is a beautiful greyhound here that looks astoundingly like Lanta. We have seen greyhounds all along the way and they are used by the Kazaks not, as one might think, for catching hares and rabbits, but for catching foxes. They say that the price of a good greyhound is as high as that of a good horse. They seem the only dainty graceful things about this rough country and among these rough people. Some of the children are sweet and gentle, but they are grubby dirty beside the greyhounds, who always look clean.

February 13

I walked again yesterday, not for long at a time. My clothes are too hampering. But long enough to get far ahead of the sledges and have the thrill of feeling completely alone in a wide, white world. No sign of life, never any sign of life but the occasional silent strings of sledges piled with bales of cotton in lovely homespun brown and tan-striped sacking, and only one train of them all yesterday.

The sunset turned the snow into a sea of opal. We went from two till dark, rested till one, and went again till dawn. Dawn was in Sergiopol, the first town on the road and halfway to Chuguchak.

I had counted the hours to Sergiopol, not only because it marked half the journey done, but because I hoped it might hold something better than a dirty Kazak hut and that I might be able to wash and change my clothes. So I wanted to weep when, after driving through bare streets of clean little Russian log houses, we turned in at the same kind of filthy pigsty we'd found at every tiny village.

Kitaiski has often remarked that our drivers are infallible in their knack of picking the dirtiest corner of every village. "But those foreigners," he would say deprecatingly, "they don't know clean from dirty." It was true, they didn't, and it never occurred to them that I might mind the squalor or long to wash my face. They had been reluctant in the first place to take a woman along, but, having accepted me, they treated me as one of them. I liked that and would not for worlds have been a poor sport about it. They did do little extra things to make me comfortable and always gave me the best place to sleep, but nevertheless it was a communistic group and I could picture their scorn if I tried to put on any extra airs like face washing.

They always shared their food with me, so I shared mine with them. Naturally their lusty appetites made short work of the little I had brought, so that I have been living with them on sour, coarse, frozen bread, bad tea, and hunks of boiled mutton.

So the Sergiopol hut seemed worse than usual. All the town came to stare at the strange foreign woman, and, being town folk, were sophisticated. The Kazaks often remind me of the gypsies who used to camp on our corner lots at home, the women especially, with their dirty cotton clothes, full ruffled skirts, tight jackets, and gay kerchiefs, their dark skins and barbaric jewelry. And they beg like gypsies, too. They beg for my bread, my tea, money, my bracelet. And they are dreadful thieves. Kitaiski is always warning me to watch my belongings, and all the way along our men have taken turns guarding the sleighs and horses day and night.

February 15

Misfortune again. The horse on my sledge has been about to die for two days. He keeps falling down all the time and it gives me the creeps. He has the colic, and

45

they have tried all their cures, strangling him and sticking him with needles and beating him, and he gets worse all the time. One good point—they've taken all the cargo off my sledge, so it has only me to pull, and I've been able to stretch out for the first time.

At four yesterday, after a day of snowing and blowing and the horse dying, we came to our first trees in all the eleven days—a clump of elms. That was a real thrill. But the hut where we stayed was, if possible, the filthiest yet, just big enough for us all to get in, hot and smelly and crawling with lice.

We ate more greasy mutton and expected to get on by midnight, but the poor old horse got worse and couldn't walk, so we had to stay till morning. There wasn't room for everyone to lie down and the house was so stuffy and crawly that I ventured to try sleeping in my sledge. It was terrifically cold, but freezing to death seemed to be preferable to being eaten and suffocated in a smelly, smoky room of dirty men, all of whom snored or coughed or spit or scratched.

I have had a queer kind of pleasure out of suffering from the filth and squalor and discomfort of this trip. It is so awful that it's funny. And in a way it's rather glorious. I like knowing I can have a grand time in spite of it. And it's glorious because it's real and human. It's all "experience." I can't explain it exactly, but it seems a great experience to me. And I think I'll never be squeamish about anything again. I'm sure a good many of our "sensibilities" are very artificial.

Well, I *was* cold sleeping in the cart, and when they dug me out in the morning there was an inch or two of snow all over me. But at least I was clean and didn't itch.

February 16

At last even Kitaiski has rebelled against the filthy places where we have been stopping. He turned back at the door of the one today, saying that he was going to find a cleaner place for us to stay. And sure enough he did, and he and I have now set up housekeeping in a comparatively sweet and pleasant little house. I have had a good wash, the first for days. We have had Chinese tea he fished out of his bag and some dates and sweet chocolate I fished out of mine, and he is feeling very pleased with himself that his sensibilities are fine enough to appreciate cleanliness. "Those dirty Russians," says he, "don't know the difference."

Alas, Five Kopecks has just come to tell us we are leaving at six. This is the shortest stop we've made yet, just because we have a nice place for once. How really ironical!

Turkestan Reunion

A sunny day yesterday, and the country is getting hilly, rugged hills, so that, all covered with snow, they look like real mountains. We went from one till after sunset and I walked a lot. A young moon was lighting the snow palely when we stopped. I'd love to have gone on all night. But I ate mountains of bread and tea and went to sleep. Kitaiski wakened me at one to "eat meat." I can't care for large amounts of tasteless mutton in the middle of the night, but I drank two bowls of soup. And at 2:30 we started again.

Such a road I've never seen nor dreamed of. It got worse and worse, till by morning we were just floundering along. There was deep powdery snow and underneath it holes in the road as high as your head. There was one stretch of half a mile along a hillside that took us four hours. In eight hours we had made about two miles. The horses were always falling into drifts to their necks and the sledges tumbling quite over, and it took ages to dig them out. It was all I could do to get myself over that stretch, one step snow to my ankles and the next step to my hips. I scrambled along with feet and hands both and was worn out when we arrived at three—over twelve hours on the way and only sixteen miles. The horses are worn out, too, and if there is much more road like this we'll never get to Chuguchak. We are in a nasty little hole of a hut now and will probably have to rest the beasts till morning.

Sledge drivers lead a wonderful life, dealing with each day as it comes, never seeming to care where they go or how long it takes them, much less where they sleep or what they have to eat.

Another horse died today. Makes me feel like Sven Hedin crossing the Himalayas. They have readjusted the loads and put the cargo back on my sledge, so that now I have less room than ever.

Real style in Kazak gentlemen's headgear seems to be a sort of flowered calico bonnet that ties under the chin and is lined with thick white fur that frames their brown faces and decidedly detracts from the fierce appearance one expects them to have. They swagger about in their sheepskin suits, bright sashes, and high leather boots, with their fierce clucking noises, and all the time they look like gentle little rabbits because of their white fur bonnets. The bonnets are a great mistake. The women wear various versions of what look like old-fashioned high-necked nightdresses.

Mutton tonight was more tough and tasteless than ever, but the men licked their fingers with the usual relish. The biggest driver, a sort of fee-fi-fo-fum individual, always cracks the bones open with a hatchet and sucks out the marrow with as loud noises as possible.

Turkestan Reunion

Curiouser and curiouser. I seem suddenly to have been deposited in a picture-book Russian cottage and left here with no one I ever saw before. Just why I am here and how long I am to stay and what's to happen next remains to be seen. Meanwhile it is very entertaining.

We rode all day in a whirling snowstorm, the kind where you can't see the horse's tail in front of your face, and about three we drove into what might have been a town if one could have seen it, and into a sort of yard. One of the drivers appeared out of a swirl of snow and brought me in here and I've seen none of them since. That was three hours ago.

I discovered myself in a two-roomed cottage with a huge white plaster stove, mud floors, and little ruffled curtains at the windows. A merry old woman and two young girls rushed to take off my snow-caked coat and cap and boots and mittens and bring me water to wash with. Then they started the samovar and soon I was sitting at a table with a homespun cloth, devouring a great bowl of *borsch* and hunks of black bread and boiled eggs and tea with cream in it. Nothing ever tasted so good as the eggs and cream.

The cottage is neat as a pin and has plants growing in tin cans on all the window sills. The girls have long braids and print kerchiefs and long dresses, and are knitting by the window and singing Russian songs.

This has been the wildest day of all. We started at three this morning and battled twelve hours with the road and made less distance than we did yesterday.

After my horse died they gave me an erratic mare who had upset more loads than all the other horses put together. She is such a dumb-bell. She sees that the road looks rough whereas on either side of the road the deep unbroken snow is as level and smooth as can be. Every few minutes she is tempted to try it and of course she goes into a drift to her neck and has to be hauled out by the tail, with much struggling and beating. We have only five drivers for our fourteen sledges and they walk along at intervals and try to guide the horses by yelling at them. The driver and I both yelled ourselves hoarse at that fool mare this morning, but it didn't seem to have much effect. And I was getting cold and the snow was beginning to get down my neck and run in icy rivulets, so I decided to retire under cover and pray.

I had been under cover only about five minutes, bouncing and jouncing around, when all of a sudden I found myself face down in a snowdrift with my belongings on top of me. After that I begged some rope from a driver and made some reins and have been driving the nag myself all day. It has worked very well, except that she has a hard mouth and I consequently have a lame arm. I ought to be drawing wages for this trip.

Driving meant that I had to perch precariously on the front of the sledge in the snow. It is the heaviest, wettest snow we have had and I got caked all over, thicker and thicker, including my face. My coat remained fairly waterproof, but the scarf around my neck got saturated and little rivers of ice ran down inside my clothes. It isn't as bitter cold today as it has been, but I was well chilled when we arrived.

Today Kitaiski rebelled again. I love to see Kitaiski rebel—it relieves my feelings so. It takes a lot to make him do it, but when he gets worked up to it he is a man of action. He told me this morning that we should get to a village today—I suppose that is where we are now—and that here he would hire a good sleigh and take me to Bakti on the Turkestan border in two days. If we stay with our match caravan it will take at least five.

He talked a great deal about what a good fellow he was and how he knew I wanted to get there soon. I suggested that he was probably eager to get there too. "Oh, no," said he, "fast or slow is all the same to me, but a few dollars more or less doesn't make any difference and I'll take you on if you want me to."

In later conversation, however, it developed that the consul at Semipalatinsk had given him a month to make the round trip to Chuguchak, and that if he had to spend all the time on the road he wouldn't have any time with his friends there. So this isn't entirely a Boy-Scout move on his part. He had honestly thought we should make the trip in nine or ten days. He had told me that he had traveled this road many times, but it appears he had never done it before in the winter.

Now I am wondering if he has given me the slip and gone his own way. The snow is still coming down in clouds. It looks as if we were snowed in here for weeks and I'm only sixty-five miles from Owen. I could go quite mad thinking about that.

7 P.M.

The blessed Kitaiski finally did appear, covered with snow, to ask if I really did want him to hire us a good sleigh to take us on tomorrow. I told him I most certainly did. The sledges we came in are about wrecked now. One of them fell all to pieces today. And we couldn't go slower; so, while I don't entirely believe in Kitaiski, we can't really lose by changing.

He talked big, of course, about how he had a lot of Chinese friends here and they all begged him to stay with them a few days and said he really shouldn't go on in all this snow, but he told them that he had an American woman in his charge who was quite helpless without him and that her husband was waiting for her in Chugu-chak and it would be *pu hao kan* (not good looking) if he didn't give up his good times with his friends and take me all the way. So I told him he was a good boy and he's gone off now to hire the sleigh, which I won't count on until I see it, as, what with the weather and the roads, it may not be so simple.

I just discovered a small boy on top of the stove, lying on his tummy eating sunflower seeds.

February 20

It is snowing again this morning, hard, and I could weep.

Kitaiski showed up again last night to say that we might be able to go this afternoon if it stopped snowing. We have gone every day until now in the snow, but I suppose there is a limit to how deeply the roads can be buried and still be possible.

This is a sweet cottage. We had a supper last night of tea and black bread, sour cream, salt fish, salt pork, and pickles. The old couple insisted on giving me their big wooden bed, and two of the drivers slept on the floor beside me. The family slept in layers on the stove and the other drivers stayed at an inn. The old lady was up at five making bread. We had a kind of stew for breakfast made of dough boiled with potatoes and a little salt pork. I wish I could walk to Chuguchak.

As I was writing just now I heard a great shrieking and yelling outside and looked out of the window to see men tearing down the street on horses, with great sticks and clubs in their hands, and men, women, and children pouring after them, calling excitedly. It looked like the entire town. And just as I was dying of curiosity to know what it was all about Kitaiski appeared and told me they were driving a wolf out of town.

The old lady is spinning in a corner at a spinning wheel, mark of advanced civilization. All the spinning I have seen on the road has been done on a twirling stick.

February 21

All the town came to see me yesterday—first two officials for my passport, then a dressy Kirghiz gentleman with a snappy little mustache, and then a whole sewing circle of apple-cheeked girls in white kerchiefs. Finally, about two, up drove Kitaiski with two sledges and announced that we were going, and I realized that it had stopped snowing at last and the sun was breaking through the clouds. And out of the window I saw appear a whole town of little white plaster houses and green domes of a church and people coming out of their houses after the storm and ploughing through the snow-filled streets.

The old lady rushed around and fed us soup and cold fish and gave me a fresh loaf of bread for the journey. And after much packing and roping and paying off our old drivers we were off at four.

Kitaiski had produced two sledges, one for us and one for our belongings. A Tatar driver drove the luggage and Kitaiski stowed me in the back of our sledge, on the bed rolls, and squatted in front to drive it himself, feeling very important and pleased with himself.

We had a felt rigged up on branches to canopy us and looked very stylish. And the road was much better than it had been. There were stretches where the horses could almost trot.

We reached a Kazak hut at nine and stayed there till four in the morning. The most attractive Kazak woman I have seen yet climbed out of bed to make us tea. She made the usual coy remarks about Kitaiski and me and offered us her bed. How did I dare travel without my husband and with another man? Kitaiski explained that it was because we were both "educated," which was a little beyond her comprehension.

I get awfully annoyed at not being able to talk. There are so many things I want to know. Of course, traveling with six men, not being able to talk with them has been in a way a protection, especially against a good many embarrassing conversations. They are pretty crude animals and the Kazak women in the huts where we have stopped are certainly not much in the way of chaperons. They seem to be completely unmoral creatures.

I had heard of travelers being embarrassed by the hospitality of Kazak households which pressed upon them the services of their women and were offended if they were not accepted, and that almost any Kazak woman, was considered to be at the disposal of the passing traveler, and from bits I did understand of the conversations of the drivers I can well believe this to be true.

While we were drinking tea at two in the morning, just before our start, Kitaiski asked me if I had heard this woman chattering to him in the night. It seemed that he, the protector of my virtue, had suggested getting into bed with her but that she had refused to let him, saying at first that it was the fast of Ramazan and it was against her religion. He had tried to persuade her that it wouldn't matter as her man was away and wouldn't know she had broken the fast, but much to his surprise she still refused to have him. Finally she confessed that she was feeling hurt because he had said that I was "educated" and then was treating her as if she weren't. But later she melted and said that if he would wait till after I had gone it wouldn't matter. Kitaiski says that everyone knows that any Kazak woman will take any traveler to bed with her and he was amazed at this woman's spirit.

Turkestan Reunion

We reached here at nine, "here" being the home of our driver, a white plaster house heavily beamed but furnished inside much like the Kazak huts. His wife has three children, a three-day-old baby, a cute small boy who looks like his father, and a yellow-haired, blue-eyed little girl who looks like hospitality to a Russian traveler.

The driver had promised to get us to Bakti on the Turkestan border tonight, but home seems to be proving too inviting, as it is now after noon and we still have forty miles to go.

Our new sledges have no bells. I miss them.

Bakti

February 22

The Turkestan border at last, and only twelve miles across the border is Chuguchak. After all, Chuguchak is probably an ordinary little town. Its importance has assumed ridiculously undue proportions in my mind ever since the day in Peking when this reunion was arranged, and has increased in magnitude during the months of waiting for the wireless message which would set the date for me to start; and as the difficulties of the journey have accumulated it has assumed the significance of a Mecca or a Jerusalem or a rainbow's end.

Turkestan Reunion

And now that I am almost there I have a sinking fear. Perhaps the journey's end will be an anticlimax after all, and my pot-of-gold husband not arrived. So I'm trying not to be too excited. But it is exciting. And how can Kitaiski be so casual? He has gone off now to find us another sleigh, as the ones we have are not allowed to cross the border.

Bakti is a fair-sized town, and I hoped vainly to the end that here I might clean up a bit for Chuguchak, having changed no clothes and scarcely washed for sixteen days. But here we have still the inevitable one-room Kazak house with much too large an audience for anything of the sort.

Even yet I don't dare count on reaching my journey's end tonight. There are still two possible obstacles to delay me: the Russian border officials, for my visa has expired, and the Turkestan border officials, for foreigners are none too welcome in that stronghold of the Middle Ages and I don't know yet how Owen has been received.

It is silly how I always think of Chuguchak as my "journey's end" when really it is only the beginning. But all the difficulties of the little-traveled roads through Turkestan and across the Himalayas, and even the trips we are planning that no white woman has done before, seem so simple when I'll be no longer a "woman traveling alone."

Turkestan Reunion

I must mail these letters to you quickly while I still have an envelope large enough to contain them, and I hope you'll read the last one first to know that I am here.

There were two impatient hours at the Russian customs while the officials looked at everything I owned. They'd never seen so many nice and interesting things before and had to ask a great many questions. I even put on a demonstration of how solidified alcohol burns. But there was no trouble about either my things or my expired visa.

Then we trotted out across the snow fields to the Gate of Turkestan, which was a wrecky-looking *pai-lou* of un-painted crumbling wood across the road between two ramshackle shanties. We went into one of the shanties, a small room full of what looked like ordinary Chinese coolies all chattering and drinking tea. One of them, at a table, seemed to be able to read and write, for he in-spected our documents and asked many questions and exhibited the queer American passport to all his pals, who tried four ways up to read the words and then de-cided they were foreign characters; then he remembered he had orders to admit me.

Then two hours across snow fields toward black and white mountains at the foot of which was Chuguchak.

Turkestan Reunion

Then into muddy streets, and Kitaiski scouting about to discover if Owen was there, while I waited perched on the loaded sleigh, and Owen coming round the corner— and there was Chuguchak.

CHAPTER III. *On life in Chuguchak, of Moses, and of how the three of us set out in a covered cart which always got stuck in the mud. Of how we crossed "Old Wind Mouth Pass" and encountered nomad Mongols and Kazaks who were all in the midst of their early spring migrations.*

T'o Li, Sinkiang

March 28, 1927

DEAREST FAMILY,

W E are jogging blissfully along on the road from Chuguchak to Urumchi, and traveling with a husband is a lot more fun than traveling alone. We have done three stages in five days and it doesn't seem to matter whether we ever arrive anywhere or not.

I wrote you from Chuguchak. I can't remember what except that I had arrived intact. In fact I don't seem to remember as much as I should about Chuguchak. It all seems one glorious blur of excitement at being with Owen again and exhilaration at having achieved what so many people had thought was impossible, not only our respective journeys but actually meeting after them at so vague a spot in the middle of Asia. I felt like a maiden in a fairy tale, who after fighting dragons, slaying monsters, struggling through impossible obstacles, quicksands, walls of ice, tangles of forest, came to the castle in the enchanted land where she found her true love at last. For after that long month of Siberian ice and snow, when I was so bitter cold and lonely for so

65

many days, and hungry and flea-bitten and afraid, I found myself suddenly in a new and different world, enchanting if not enchanted.

Even the name of it was perfectly impossible. Chuguchak! It had been a spot on the map, and then a goal, the end of a rainbow, and always as unreal as the long, cold, white days I had spent in struggling toward it. It was just another mud village in a waste of snow. But it was Turkestan. The first faint hint of spring was in the air and the noon sun was turning the streets into a sea of mud through which splashed swarms of jaunty Asiatics in a brilliant pageant of color.

Owen had been in Chuguchak for nearly a month. The Soviet consul in Urumchi, the capital, had assured him that when he reached Chuguchak he would be given a visa so that he could go on to Semipalatinsk to meet me. But it had happened just as I had feared when I didn't find him there. Between Owen's departure from Urumchi and his arrival in Chuguchak our treatment of their ambassadress to Mexico had quite rightfully annoyed them. They would give no visas to Americans, particularly not to an American who wanted to enter their territory at so remote a point as Bakti.

Daily visits to the Soviet consul had proved of no avail. He was sympathetic. He blamed it all on Moscow. He invited Owen to play chess with him. But he produced no visa.

Turkestan Reunion

The consul offered to send messages to me in Semi-palatinsk. Owen sent several, but the wires were down in many places because of the heavy snow, and if telegrams ever arrived it was after I had left. The telegram I sent to Owen from Semipalatinsk, however, through the Soviet consul, did get through, so that for seventeen days he knew that I was on my way. He knew, too, that the journey was supposed to take ten days, so that by the seventeenth his red beard was on the point of turning gray. Though fortunately for the beard he couldn't know quite how cold and bleak and difficult that journey was.

I found Owen installed with Moses in a little house belonging to a Chinese trading firm.

I must introduce Moses without further ado, as he is a very important member of the party. At a tender age Moses was a Boxer. Perhaps it is out of deference to our feelings that he claims that he always managed to stay at home on the days when there were to be any killings. When he was seventeen he went to South Africa with a labor corps to work in the mines, learned a little English, advanced himself to being an interpreter, did a bit of trading on the side and came home with $3,000, which his elder brothers promptly appropriated and squandered in short order. It was in South Africa that some facetious Englishman endowed him with the name of Moses.

He then worked up and down the land as waiter on a dining car, bar boy in a hotel, and servant to a traveling

Englishman, until he fell in with the Lattimores some fifteen years ago and has been with one or another of them ever since.

He is a huge, square fellow, looks more like a burly Negro than a Chinese, and has the most poker face I have ever seen on anyone. Except on the rare occasions when he has had too much to drink, his features are immovable and bafflingly inexpressive, which gives him an advantage over us all. He is not phenomenal as a chef or lady's maid, but is perfect as diplomat and general manager, which after all is more important. We all do what he says.

We hadn't the least intention of bringing Moses on this expedition. He was fat and forty with a wife and child in Tientsin, and we assumed that he would prefer to stay with the flesh pots of a treaty port. But not a bit of it. He knew perfectly well that traveling in the interior was ticklish business in these days of civil wars and bandits and he was coming along to look after us. So come he has, through fire and flood, always managing to conjure eggs from a wilderness and melons from a desert, to cook a dinner over three bits of camel dung, to entertain us when we are desolate and to lie fluently to get us out of a hole. And what he lacks in natural beauty he makes up in shaving.

Owen, on the other hand, has acquired a fearsome red beard which he flaunts shamelessly. He grew it perforce

during his four months of desert travel, and is quite convinced that it completes or adds to his personality in some
very desirable manner. At least it fits the landscape and
makes him into just the kind of bearded lord and master
one should achieve in Chuguchak.

Chuguchak seemed excitingly picturesque. Even without a honeymoon aura it would have been exciting. It is
Asia—not the restrained and often neurasthenic old Asia
of the China coast, but a more primitive and exuberant
Asia which tumbles out onto the streets at the first feel
of spring. Kazaks in rakish fur bonnets cavort through
the slush on shaggy ponies. Mongols in sheepskins and
purple sashes plod by on tall camels. Chantos and T'ung-
kans in high red and black leather boots drive jingling
little sledges. A long high wagon jogs by carrying a whole
family of apple-cheeked Russians wrapped in shawls. A
two-wheeled ox cart lumbers through the city gate, the
driver riding on the back of the ox and singing lustily.
Swagger and merriment everywhere, and no one walks
if he can ride. We loved the market-place and the funny
little streets lined with tall bare poplars blotched with big
black birds' nests and the curly toy gates of the toy city
wall. The country all about the town was lovely, too, still
deep in snow, great fields of it stretching to the foot of
jagged black and white mountains.

We lived in a very aristocratic Chinese inn, or rather it
was a business firm with accommodation for travelers

who were specially recommended to them. Its manager was a new rich and very rich Tientsin man, a notorious rascal with an astounding collection of villainies to his credit. He was nice to us, however, and gave us his private summer home to live in, a new little house far back of the inn and the stables with a wide garden of its own and a grove of trees, beyond which were the curving roofs of a temple with sweet bells. It was heated with a Russian stove as well as by a fire in the *k'ang,* or sleeping platform, so we were snug and happy.

One of the proud possessions of the firm was an immense black stallion almost twice the size of the local ponies and therefore considered very elegant. It champed along the muddy streets tossing its long mane and dragging after it a tiny baby-carriage sleigh at a precarious angle and only prevented from capsizing by a lank Kirghiz driver, the only man in town who could manage the beast at all. This equipage was in great and constant demand for paying formal calls. Mr. Wang would borrow it to call on Mr. Li and Mr. Li would borrow it for a return call on Mr. Wang. We used it to call on the Bogoslavskies and Owen used it to call on the governor.

The governor was wonderful, a real frontiersman. One finds few Chinese like him on the coast. He was big and bluff and hearty and said to be an excellent administrator. In fact we heard it whispered that he might some day succeed to the governorship of the province, a post which requires a giant autocrat if any ever did.

The day after Owen called on him we were just starting out for a walk when who should come prancing through our gate but a great array of mounted soldiers with none less than the governor himself riding behind them and looking immense on his little red-blanketed pony. He paid us a very friendly call and seemed to enjoy looking at guns and field glasses and cameras. He had returned only a few days before from a journey to Kulja to visit his parents, riding horseback over a difficult mountain road instead of traveling by cart as any other Chinese official would have done, by the longer but easier road. And what was more surprising, his little daughter rode with him instead of traveling, like other officials' daughters, in a closely curtained cart.

The Bogoslavskies, rather dull Russians to whom we had an introduction, showered us with attentions. They had been stranded in Chuguchak, cast up by the tide of fugitives from revolution, still with a little money and nothing to do but intrigue futilely and attempt pathetically to keep a "genteel" tone to their social life with their few *emigré* neighbors. She was fat and frizzed her hair and was insatiable in her desire to know whether or not each separate garment she wore was "in the mode." She was deliciously thrilled about our honeymoon and took coy delight in treating us as bride and groom.

Turkestan Reunion

Staying at the firm where we were was a Chinese official with a new and expensive concubine he had just brought from the coast. He had been on the governor's staff for years and was returning from a mission to Peking. The cautious governor, fearing he might have been contaminated during his absence, was detaining him on the frontier for several weeks, until he could be "politically fumigated," so to speak. Owen, though his papers had been quite in order, had been similarly held in a filthy little military post on the frontier between Mongolia and Turkestan, a prisoner for two weeks which might have been longer if he hadn't succeeded in sneaking out a message to an official friend inside who effected his release.

The concubine came to call on me, pattering through the mud in gay flowered satin shoes and coat, attended by a soldier who peeked at us through a crack in the door. She was a charming little creature and was much thrilled when we fed her coffee, foreign style.

After a fortnight of blissful laziness in Chuguchak, which gave me a chance to recover leisurely from Siberia where I had accumulated dirt, lice, and a great weariness, we began to take an interest in all Turkestan at our feet and talk of plans. What we have been wanting to do is to follow the ancient trade routes of Turkestan, along which we knew that life could be little different now from the days of the great Khans and long before the Khans, so that it would be easy to people them with the ancient caravans which bore silks and tea from China to Central Asia and the West. We want to travel like vagabonds, wandering through the province as simply and inconspicuously as possible, living as much as possible "off the country" and as the natives do, both because it is cheaper and more carefree and because we can learn more of the people and the country by doing it that way. But we have to compromise to a certain extent between our idea of the kind of people we are and the Chinese idea of the kind of people we ought to be. This is all because the Chinese officials have their own notions as to how bona fide Western travelers ought to travel, and anyone trying to act like a gypsy is likely to be harried as a Russian refugee and suspected as a spy.

Russians swarmed over the Siberian border during the Revolution, and those who didn't have enough money to get on to China or India or enough resourcefulness to support themselves in Turkestan turned beggars and made themselves a general nuisance in the towns along the main road. So a white man is no longer treated as a Lord of Creation just because he is white, and it seems that now, to be treated with any sort of respect and consideration one must make it obvious that one is not a Russian.

Most Chinese are completely unable to understand anyone's enjoying travel for its own sake. They look upon it as a necessary hardship and usually do it very badly. They wear the same clothes and carry the same flowered quilts and white embroidered pillow covers when they travel that they use at home. And if we wear corduroy breeches and khaki shirts and carry army blankets it is because we are poor and have no manners and are therefore not worthy of respect or consideration. And without the respect and consideration of Chinese officials and innkeepers we wouldn't be able to travel at all. So we are trying to atone for our khaki shirts and our lack of embroidered pillow covers by displaying all the guns, cameras, field glasses, barometer, thermos bottles and other grandeur that we have, and otherwise traveling like the most respectable of Chinese officials.

This involves my riding like a perfect Chinese lady in a springless cart discreetly curtained in blue and white. Moses and the driver sit in front of me, one on each shaft with their feet dangling over the edge, and Owen rides ahead on a handsome black pony he bought in Urumchi. And besides all this we have official escorts, civil and military. This may impress you. But you should see them to believe them.

The escorts are nominally to protect us, and probably actually to keep an eye on what we are up to, but they give us face and a good deal of information and assistance. It is difficult, however, to think of them as soldiers.

Sinkiang soldiers are something to write about. The

first specimen I saw I mistook for a beggar and they all look like hungry ragamuffins. They wear rakish dirty sheepskin caps, their clothes are made of the cheapest kind of cotton cloth and are always dirty and in rags, and they look what most of them are, degraded wrecks of humanity, for no one with any opinion of himself at all would be a soldier if he could help it. They are paid less than a bare living and must pick up all sorts of odd jobs that no one else will do in order to have enough to eat.

Our military escort turned out at first to be but one soldier. And our civil escort didn't turn up at all till two days after we had left.

When we wanted to start from Chuguchak there were no carts to be had and an inn full of passengers waiting to make the trip, and no one knew how long we'd have to wait. But after a while a cart turned up and it was generally agreed that it be allotted to take us to Urumchi. Or rather it was only the carter who turned up, as he couldn't bring his cart in through the snow and had left it at an inn a day's journey away. The trip to Urumchi is supposed to take twelve or thirteen days and he has agreed to make it for 155 taels including 15 taels for feeding and caring for Owen's pony. An Urumchi tael is worth about twenty cents gold.

We left Chuguchak on March 23rd, traveling the first day in a sleigh. It was a long white ride and though we were stuck for an hour in a little melting river we reached

Turkestan Reunion

Ho Shang, 160 li, by dark. We stopped at a big dirty inn where they swept out a little hole of a room, mostly *k'ang,* for us, and after a smoky attempt at a fire Moses made our supper with sternos and we went to bed on the *k'ang.*

The object of most travelers being to travel fast, the object of most carters is to travel slow, thereby showing that they have the upper hand. Before we went to bed the first night our carter announced that he must spend the next day fixing the big covered cart in which we were to travel the rest of the way. We demurred, not that we minded spending a day there but for the moral effect on the carter. But he won and has seemed to win ever since, the real reason probably being that we don't really care when we get to Urumchi and so can't properly fool the carter into thinking that we do.

The cart took only an hour to fix. But the carter and Owen are both in the same position. They'll have to travel slowly if their horses are to get there at all. For Owen's pony turns out to be not as husky as he is handsome and went lame on the trip up. And whereas our cart is elegant enough it has the wreckiest-looking three horses in the province.

The next morning we were up at three and off by five in order to cover as much as possible of the frozen road before the sun was high enough to melt it into rivers of mud, and as we bumped and jolted out of the village the dawn was just warming the snowy fields and mountains with a delicious glow of rose and lavender.

Our cart is beautiful, a four-wheeled wooden wagon canopied with a felt on an arched frame of rough willow wands and curtained and awninged in front with blue and white figured cotton. Our luggage is stacked at the back and in front of it I sprawl on furs and sleeping bags and with difficulty persuade Moses and the carter to leave the curtains open as no modest woman should, so that I can see where we are going.

It is called a *t'ai ch'e* (stage cart), or more commonly a *ssu-ku-lu-ch'e* (four-wheeled cart), and is the fastest thing used on these roads. Its fore wheels are smaller than its hind wheels which, in some way I don't understand, increases momentum so that on a good road three ponies can pull it at a jog trot all day long, easily covering fifty or sixty miles a day at an average of five miles an hour.

It is fairer to give these distances in li than in miles, as a mile isn't always three li. Distances are measured here as they are in China proper, not by actual measurement but by the time and effort it takes to cover them. That is, ten li going up hill are shorter than ten li going down, and a li on a bad road is shorter than one on a good road. So that a *t'ai ch'e* may continue to travel fifteen li an hour when some hours it is making four miles and some hours six.

The only other type of wagon used on this road is a *ta ch'e* (big cart). It is perched high on two huge wheels, travels much more slowly than a *t'ai ch'e,* and is usually used for goods rather than passengers, being pulled by from one to five horses according to its load.

For our first day of cart travel the snow was deep and wet and tired the horses and the cart was always sticking in the mud. Once we got stuck completely, and that was where we found our civil escort. The cart was in mud and snow to the axles and almost tipped over. "In fact this cart counts as tipped over," the carter announced philosophically, and he continued to beat the poor old horses in the vain hope that they could struggle out. I held their ponies while Owen and our soldier helped Moses push and dig and pry and the carter ploughed around and beat the horses, stopping occasionally to remark cheerfully, "Ai ya, my cart is ruined."

Everyone's feet were very wet when two fur-bonneted Kazaks rode up on ponies. The Kazaks are swagger fellows. In this district they are Kirei Kazaks, a different tribe from the ones I lived with in Siberia, and they wear their fur bonnets at a rakish angle which makes them look quite fierce and not at all rabbity as they do in Semipalatinsk. These two dismounted and I held their ponies, too, while they helped prod.

Their added strength did the deed, and I had climbed back into my retreat when I heard a great moaning and wailing at the rear, just where I couldn't see what was happening. Soon Owen came to report that one of our Kazak rescuers had just stolen a pony right out from under a passing tribesman, whereupon the poor wretch lay flat out on the snow and began to wail and moan at the top of his lungs.

Our soldier went back to mediate and much to our amazement the thief unfolded documents to prove that he had been sent by the *hsien yamen* (civil administration) of the village we had just left to escort us halfway to Urumchi. He had an order to commandeer ponies when he needed them and explained that his wailing victim's pony had not been stolen but only commandeered. As he already had one horse to ride the soldier persuaded him to return it and come along behind us, which he has been doing ever since. One more to house and feed and tip, but he is merry enough and ought to supply us with interesting bits about the home life of the Kazaks as he speaks Chinese quite well.

Early in the afternoon we reached a few Kazak huts on a windy sweep of rolling country and we stopped for the night in a house much like the ones on the road from Semipalatinsk but larger and more comfortable. Moses, soldiers, carters and all of us slept in one room with a large family. Two babies squalled all the time they weren't being fed. In the middle of the night I woke to see two tousled women creeping from their beds. The dim light from the dying coals of the supper fire gleamed on long brown arms as they struggled into their red cotton gowns. One lit a wick in a broken saucer of oil as the other added bits of dry dung to the fire and set over it an iron kettle hung from a tripod. Great golden rounds of bread were set in the ashes to warm and when tea was made they roused the others stealthily so as not to waken their guests and sat silently about the fire eating their Ramazan night meal. The Kazaks are Mohammedans and so can't eat by day during this month, which is called the fast of Ramazan.

This tiny village was the last stop before Lao Feng K'ou, the famous windy pass, literally "old wind mouth," where in a high wind a man is unable even to stand and many have been frozen to death. It was here that the new postal commissioner and his wife, going to Urumchi a few months ago, were caught by a storm and their cook was nearly frozen in the snow. The poor chap lost both of his hands. Carters are usually unwilling to start through the pass if there is the least cloud in the sky.

It scarcely looks like a pass at all but more like a wide valley, as the ascent to the crest is very gradual and it would not be in the least difficult if it were not for the wind. The Chuguchak side of it is supposed to be the most dangerous, and though we had a clear day for it it took us the whole of it, battling against the wind, to reach the little village at the crest.

Turkestan Reunion

About noon our cart got irrevocably stuck in a ditch and Owen and I rode on with the Kazak for the remaining twenty li to send back help. Just before we reached the village we came upon a wonderful encampment of nomad Mongols in the process of setting up half a hundred yurts. They weren't white yurts like the ones around Kueihua, but browns and tans almost the color of the brown fields, and they were there in all stages of construction from the erecting of the first staves to roping on the felts and setting up the iron fireplaces.

All in and out among the yurts were hundreds of camels and ponies and oxen still saddled from the journey, and flocks of sheep and goats and swarms of children playing all about. The men were tending to the animals and the women in the gayest clothes and kerchiefs and bangles and beads were busy arranging the yurts, their skirts and the yurt felts all flapping in the wind. Our Kazak sent some men on ponies back to help the carter and we vastly entertained an admiring yurtfull with our cameras. They told us they had just come up the pass from their winter quarters in the Jair Hills and reported much snow and hard going.

We stayed that night at a soldiers' barracks, where, except for a narrow passage through the center, the little room was filled by two great *k'angs*. On one of these we camped for the night, sitting cross-legged at a ten-inch-high *k'ang* table to eat our supper of canned tomatoes and spaghetti and then stretching out where we were to sleep well after a long hard day of traveling.

All the while we were eating and going to sleep we watched life on the other *k'ang*. Not more than two or three yards from our noses a small group of Chinese travelers were reclining around a tiny opium lamp enjoying long sweet smokes. Through the smoke and glow of the supper fires I watched their long fingers carefully preparing the gummy black balls and elaborately arranging their grubby blankets for the fullest possible enjoyment of the smoke. We went to sleep with the sticky sweet smell of opium in our nostrils.

I'll never forget yesterday as long as I live, for we met the people of Prester John, a long brilliant pageant of them struggling through the snow of Lao Feng K'ou on their way to new camping grounds.

I have changed my mind about nomads. I had always had a vague and naïve idea that they lived a free and idyllically simple life, wandering like the wind wherever fancy led. The first nomad migrations we have encountered, however, have disillusioned me forever.

There was no visible road, but only a long stretch of deep wet snow between far-away jagged black mountains, and all day, out of the gray distance, crept the caravans, brilliant against the dull whiteness of the snow. It was the kind of gray day which enhances the vividness of color, and their red and yellow and plum-colored clothing and saddle bags and blankets splashed a long and gorgeous pageant of color on the gray-white canvas. The men drove pony herds ahead to trample a path, then came the women with the household goods roped onto camels, and last of all the larger children driving the flocks of sheep and goats.

We were having a difficult time enough with no one to look after but ourselves and a cart to ride in. But they had no carts, and it was at the time of the spring when everything had babies. Women on ponies carried tiny babies tied into cradles on the pommels of their saddles, while new-born camels and goats and lambs and puppies and yearling children hung in bags and baskets from the backs of camels and oxen. Infant mortality on those first spring migrations must be appalling, but migrate they must, to the pastures where the first grass is, in the spring, or their animals will die, and the lives of all of them depend upon their animals.

We waited on the narrow trail while they struggled and tumbled past us or turned off into the deep snow to file at a snail's pace across the white fields, and the moving of a whole community seemed appallingly difficult and complicated.

You can't imagine how weary we were last night when well after dark we staggered into a tiny one-room inn huddling solitary in the midst of the vast expanse of snow. A fire of tamarisk boughs burned merrily in a crude stove in the center of a square low-raftered room of putty-colored mud, its only furniture a soft brown felt on the floor, cross-barred in irregular cream-colored stripes, and a tall cream-colored candle flickering against the far wall. Moses and the cart were lost, and while Owen went back to look for them I curled up in a corner in my sheepskin coat. Strange men wandered in and out, Chantos and Kazaks, to look at the foreign woman, to warm themselves and make tea at the fire or have a snooze in the corner beyond the stove. A smarty fellow tried to talk to me in Russian. Then the lost ones turned up, so exhausted that I cooked the supper, corn and sausages, on the inn fire and we tumbled into our sleeping bags, only too glad that the presence of other travelers prevented our undressing.

CHAPTER IV. *Of pleasant adventures in a covered wagon, of Tientsin men and inns and of how we found spring in Urumchi.*

DEAR FAMILY,

YESTERDAY and today we have been traveling through bad bandit country but as this isn't bandit season we haven't met a one.

Beyond T'o Li the country suddenly changed from snow fields to bare rocky hills with only streaks of snow in the crevices, and six hours on a much better road brought us to a tiny inn, one of three houses in a nest of hills. While Moses was unpacking we walked up a sunny little canyon from the inn, where Owen missed a duck and shot a grouse which made us a very good supper. Around a corner of the canyon we came upon a small Kazak encampment. Our first awareness of it was a bedlam of dogs, but we soon distinguished brown yurts against the brown stone wall of the canyon, pleasant in the late afternoon sunshine, and then a swarm of children and a woman milking a goat. A grinning chap in rough sheepskins came out to meet us and soon a crowd collected to look at our guns and peer delightedly through the field glasses.

It is in the summer that this rough hilly country is

supposed to be dangerous because of Kazak bandits. In the winter there are camps like this one all along the road and the men do not dare to rob so near their homes, for in case of a hold-up it would be simple enough to seize the head man of the nearest camp and hold him responsible for the robbery. In the summer, however, they move their camps far into the hills and the men ride down several days to the road to hold up travelers and then flee back to their far-away safe retreats.

We have met both Mongol and Kazak caravans today looking almost as brilliant against the dun hills as they did against the white snow of the pass. The effect of the Mongol caravans is gayer than that of the Kazaks because both the men and the women wear clothes of brilliant colors. But the Kazak men, though clad more somberly, have the air of being more swashbuckling and vigorous than the Mongols. In fact they look satisfactorily as nomad bandits *should* look. And their caravans have color, too, supplied by the clothing of the women and by an occasional beautiful old rug of soft reds and yellows slung over the back of a camel. It seems amazing that both of these races have lived here so many hundreds of years and mingled so little, for they seem to live the same kind of life in the same way and yet remain quite distinct in blood and language and religion.

We have been traveling along for several days with a Chinese official, ex-chief of police of Chuguchak, who is on his way to be chief of police in Urumchi. He and his wife and three children ride by day and sleep by night in one cart, a huge *ta ch'e,* in which they also carry their luggage. As the hamlet where we stayed last night had only one inn and that inn had only one room we slept in our cart, too, and Moses and the official's cook took turns at the stove.

The innkeeper and Moses fell upon each other's necks when they discovered that they hailed from near the same spot in Chihli Province. "Ai," said Moses, "I was in your home town in the Boxer year. Where were you then?"

"Oh, oh," said the innkeeper, "don't ask me that!" It seems that a lot of Chihli men are in Turkestan because they had to flee from home after the Boxer uprising. And most of them have made their fortunes here. Kansu men have been coming to Sinkiang for generations and amounted to nothing at all, but particularly since the last Chinese reconquering of Turkestan fifty years ago when the province was christened Sinkiang (Hsin Chiang, new dominion) and colonization was encouraged, men from the coast have made their way out here and grown rich in a few years. It is difficult now, however, for them to get home again, for while the governor is glad enough to have the Chinese make money in his province, he doesn't want them to take it away.

Moses gives us a lot of face by being from Tientsin. There are many Chinese in Turkestan, particularly here in the north, but any of them who do manual labor, the working classes so to speak, including servants, are all from the western provinces of Kansu and Shensi or are what is called *pen-ti jen,* local men, sons and grandsons of early Chinese colonists, or, what is more likely, of convicts exiled from China or of fugitives from justice. The prosperous merchants are from Chihli and are commonly spoken of as Tientsin men, though they may in reality come from a village some distance from Tientsin. These "Tientsin men" form a friendly clan all over the province and seem to be much respected.

So, since all Tientsin men who come to Turkestan get rich, no one but us can afford a servant from Tientsin, and dear old Mose, who gets nothing at all from us but his keep and twenty Mexican dollars a month that we pay to his family in Tientsin, has established us with a reputation.

Today we had good going again and made 140 li by three o'clock, walking for a while this morning through rugged little canyons in the hills. Just before we reached our destination the carter called excitedly to Owen that there was a wolf on the road ahead and begged him to shoot it. Owen thought that the slinking black animal they were pointing to in the scrub ahead was a dog, but the carter and Moses both insisted that it was a wolf and as their acquaintance with wolves is more extensive than Owen's he took their word for it and shot it dead, a very good hit. Then we rushed up to the body and discovered that it *was* a dog, a crossbred greyhound, and we felt rather ill, especially as it was almost sure to belong to the village where we were to spend the night and its death might cause any amount of unpleasantness. The carter nobly took all the blame, but luckily for us he discovered that the dog was a stray from some caravan.

We are staying at a little telegraph station, also with only one room and also with the official's family, so we are sleeping in the cart again tonight.

April 3

Yesterday was still and warm and we meandered through a brown gold country of clumps of stubby little trees and yellow marshes. The bells on our jogging ponies were all that broke the stillness until the soldiers spied a pheasant or a rabbit or called out to Owen that there was wild duck ahead. Then the carter would pull up his horses and Owen would clamber out with his gun. Once I followed him far across a meadow to the edge of a marsh, beyond which was a pond black with duck. They were out of range, but Owen couldn't resist a try, which filled the air with whirring wings. He shot a duck, a rabbit and two pheasant.

Turkestan Reunion

We stopped for the night at a sweet inn, a little mud-walled enclosure in the midst of the same emptiness. We went out at sunset to the edge of a marsh where ducks hid in the long grass and quacked loudly and the air was filled with the whirr of wild geese. And then we went home to rabbit stew and a good sleep in the cart.

For two days we have been traveling toward high snowy mountains glistening against the sky. They are our first sight of the T'ien Shan, the Heavenly Mountains, which we shall cross after leaving Urumchi.

I had a new and nasty experience today. The cart got stuck in a marsh and we walked on to a Chinese village. The sun was hot so I waited in the shade in front of a little tea shop while Owen went to look for a duck. As soon as he was out of sight all the village children appeared, shouting "Russian ——" (I didn't understand the second word!), and started throwing mud and stones at me. At first I tried to laugh it off, but when I saw that there were several grown ups watching them and interfering not at all I was furious, and not having enough of the local Chinese to tell them what I thought of them in any but a laughable manner, I stalked back to the cart as haughtily as I could with bits of mud and pebbles hitting me in the back. The cart was a quarter of a mile away and I wanted terribly to run, but I knew that would only make them worse, so I walked with as much dignity as I could muster, but I've never felt more foolish. Owen was furious, too, when I told him about it, and tried to send our soldiers back to give the villagers a few pointers on manners, but the soldiers wouldn't take it seriously, though the villagers Owen had been hunting with apologized profusely.

This afternoon we reached Hsi Hu, one of the two towns between Chuguchak and Urumchi, and Moses has just come in with a new supply of eggs and dried apricots and, great excitement, two yellow pears. Everything so far had been amazingly cheap. There are no fixed charges at the inns but we pay from two to five taels a day for fuel and sleeping space for the whole lot of us. And we eat such simple food that even with Moses and ourselves and the carter and two or three escorts to feed, and the escorts and innkeepers to tip, it amounts to very little. I suppose our total expenses, not counting cart hire, are less than two dollars gold a day, and we couldn't spend more if we wanted to, as Owen tips generously and there are no luxuries to be had.

Our Kazak leaves us here and is going off with a marvelous collection of old tin cans and empty bottles. Such civilized effects are so rare here that he will do a big business selling them for a tael or two apiece in the local bazaar.

It is wonderful to watch Moses tipping an innkeeper or a soldier. He squats in a corner and fumbles with his roll of tattered bills till he extracts the proper amount.

Then he rises and very impressively presents the money, saying, "The gentleman (literally "old grandfather") presents you with three taels," in a tone which plainly says, "See how beneficent he is. You have been honored in serving him."

April 5

We spent all yesterday at Hsi Hu. The carter wanted to nurse his old horses and lured us into agreeing to the delay with enthusiastic accounts of a game of *baigu* to be held at noon a few li outside of the city. It was a Mohammedan holiday, the end of the Ramazan fast, and the town was gay with carnival. All morning Chantos and Chinese, dressed in their best, filed into the inn yard paying calls. I sat in the cart much diverted with watching them while Owen was writing inside the inn, Moses was busy with yesterday's duck over a little open fire in the inn yard, and the carter was having a beautiful time taking off and putting on again the wheels of his wrecky old cart.

Moses says our carter is famous for being the best man and having the worst horses on the North Road. It seems that he always manages to get the best paying passengers and to take the longest time getting them anywhere of any of the carters. He seems to owe money everywhere and is very cheerful about it. He is supposed to be a good horse doctor and so thinks he can buy old scarecrow nags and doctor them up so they can travel, but he lost two horses on his last trip and is about to lose one on this. Moses told him if he'd sell his horses and buy machinery he might be able to make his cart go. To which he merrily replied that we may be traveling for pleasure but he is traveling for fun. He has already spent 150 of the 155 taels we are paying him for the trip but he assures us he can always run up bills.

We were very eager to see the *baigu,* the famous Chanto game where a sheep is thrown into the ring and men ride for it on horses, trying to capture it from each other. We rode out at noon with the carter but people on the street called out to us that the game was to be later in the afternoon. And when they summoned us again the luckless carter and his horses were not to be found. So we walked out, seeing a great crowd in the distance and fifty or more ponies galloping about a field. But just as we arrived the game was finished and we rather than the horsemen became the center of interest. The crowd flocked around us, excited from the game and growing more and more hoodlum. Again the curse of the Russian refugees. But we finally managed to shake the mob by turning abruptly down a steep hillside and sauntering unconcernedly away.

It is the Chinese everywhere here who seem to be the

hoodlum element. The Chantos may be rascals but they are always friendly and not over curious. However, the whole population of the province except for the small element of more substantial Tientsin business men are pretty scallywag and roughneck, the rag tags and outlaws from everywhere. It is no wonder that the governor must uphold his reputation as a fearsome autocrat and rule like a tyrant king.

Our Kazak courier has been replaced by a feeble-minded looking Chinese lad. We had become fond of our Kazak and his commandeering ways and though we had said elaborate farewells yesterday morning, when he turned up again last night after his celebration with a present of hard-boiled eggs tied up in a handkerchief we couldn't resist giving him another tip, which is exactly what he had in mind himself. Hard-boiled eggs seem to be a part of this holiday as they are of our Easter, which latter Moses says the Chinese call the "Foreign Egg Festival." The Mohammedans carry the eggs about the street and knock them against the eggs of their neighbors. The one whose egg breaks has to forfeit it to the other.

We've been twelve hours on the road today, most of it through barren gobi with the white mountains on the right and low rocky hills ahead. Just before sunset we came to this pleasant oasis of willow trees and tiny streams and a quaint village in the midst of them. As we were jogging up the tree-lined road four horsemen came suddenly galloping toward us, one with the black sheep of a *baigu* game under his arm. Just beside us the other three caught up to him and lashed at him with their whips till another of the men obtained the sheep and they galloped after him back toward the village.

April 8

Our escort has been increased to three, two wrecky-looking soldiers and the *hsien yamen* courier. The latter, a poor chinless kid, was sent off with a limping skeleton of a horse and an order to commandeer others as he needed them. But he had never commandeered a horse in his life and was afraid to try it, so he walked all day, leading his own and Owen's ponies. Today four soldiers turned up to escort us, their tongues all hanging out for tips from the foreign "old grandfather," but Moses told them confidentially that his old grandfather never tipped more than one soldier, whereupon two of them promptly disappeared.

Early yesterday afternoon we reached Manass, the other town on our road. There is a Catholic mission about three miles outside the town with a German priest whom Owen had met on his way up, and as soon as we had set up camp in the little inn room we walked out to see him. It is surprising to find any foreigner living alone so far from anywhere, and to find this particular person seemed doubly a mystery. He is a huge, good-looking fellow, an ex-artillery officer and a charming and intelligent gentleman. He came out into his little courtyard to greet us, very tall and clean in his long black Chinese gown, the open collar of which was faced with blue the color of his very blue eyes, his fresh German face topped with a gray tweed golf cap in delightful contrast to his long red beard. He called immediately to his boy to bring wine to refresh us and the little fellow soon appeared carrying a bottle almost as big as he was, full of delicious wine which the priest had made himself from grapes grown in his garden.

We sat in his little study while he smoked a big black pipe as long as his red beard and told us most entertainingly how he had come here, several months from the coast in a little Peking cart, speaking no word of Chinese and with no one to teach him. Since his arrival four years ago he has not only learned the language but has organized a hospital with drugs and instruments two years on the road from Germany, and runs an orphanage and a big farm. He showed us all his establishment, his tiny church, his wine cellar, his kitchen, his horses and his gardens. His little mud houses look from without much like those of his neighbors, but inside they are spotless and tidy. We stayed for dinner, a very good dinner, after which he sent us rattling home in a fast and funny little cart past rows of poplar trees under the new moon and through a lovely old gate with moonlight gleaming through its two round windows and its wooden fretwork.

This morning we saw the sun rise, and started through its glow on two long stages, our poor dying nag just barely able to stagger along. The carter very nearly gave up and encamped us some forty li short of our goal, but finally managed to land us at a village delightfully called "Butterfly Cup." It isn't as enchanting as it sounds. At least the inn is gloomy and windowless, but a copper pan of glowing coals has cheered our little room and we've had a good supper, a bowl of bean sprouts and mutton from a restaurant supplemented by a can of corn and Chanto bread and coffee.

April 9

We were ready before the carter this morning and walked thirty li before he caught up to us. For the last few days villages have become more frequent and food more easily procurable, as a result of which we have been starting off with only a bit of bread and tea in the early morning and stopping before noon for a "brunch" at some little village tea house. One day a bowl of *chua fan*, rice browned with bits of mutton much like Turkish *pilaf*, and one day fried eggs, but usually our own boiled eggs, Chanto bread, dried apricots and chocolate, with only tea from the restaurant. This may not sound like a delicious repast but our appetites make anything taste good. We like Chanto bread and have it for every meal. It is baked in large flat round pancakes and is golden brown and crisp.

Since leaving Manass we have seen more dead towns than live ones, as the road is lined with ruins of villages destroyed during the Mohammedan rebellion fifty years ago. Lots of land, too, that used to be irrigated is now dry.

The villages and farms in this district are for the most part inhabited by T'ung-kans, Chinese Mohammedans who came from Kansu and Shensi, though no one knows exactly what their origin is. They are supposed to be a crafty lot. Carruthers quotes a Chinese saying to the effect that "one Jew can cheat ten Christians, one Chinaman is the equal of ten Jews, but one T'ung-kan can get the better of ten Chinese."

April 10

Urumchi at last, after twenty days on the road. Owen had made the same journey in twelve. Still I rather hate it to end, even after twenty. It has been a glorious care-free gypsy journey and now we have all sorts of businesses to attend to and people who must be seen.

Last night, our last on the road, we banqueted on everything left in the food box, peas, fried eggs, onions and spaghetti. We were up before dawn and the ride today has been lovely, a fresh blue and gold morning, quaint villages, a wide view of glorious high mountains, and almost at the foot of them the Urumchi oasis, tree-lined roads, a wide river bed, gay little streets swarming with men in high boots and women in brilliant skirts, little black bodices and long black veils.

The country has been dusty now for several days, but the streets of Urumchi are rivers of black mud. Our cart couldn't get into the city at all. We climbed out at the edge of town and walked in, and Moses turned up an hour later, having brought our stuff in three small carts.

We are living at a business firm, importers of miscellaneous goods from Russia and the China coast and owned by Pan Tsi-lu, the official Owen had known in Tientsin. He has just paid us a call and is most awfully nice. The firm is overwhelming us with attentions. We have two typically Chinese rooms, stiff and whitewashed, with scrolls on the walls in neat rows and chairs and tables arranged in stiff symmetry around the edge. The inner room has a huge and lovely curtained *k'ang* for us to sleep on, but the effect is rather ruined by a foreign iron bedstead in one corner of the room.

Servants have been dancing attendance, bringing us tea and then wash water and then tea in glasses with milk and sugar in it and a fearful and wonderful collection of cakes and candy and cigarettes. And all the while various members of the firm and goodness knows who all have been coming in to pay their respects. And then we were fed a large meal. And finally, just as Owen was about to escape to a bath house to wash off three weeks' accumulation and change into city clothes, a sweet old English missionary from the China Inland Mission whom Owen had known when he was here before came over and spent the rest of the afternoon.

They have both gone now and I have been unpacking. The manager has just come in with three servants and tacked a flowered cotton blanket on the wall. We found two touching gifts in our room when we arrived, a bottle of perfume for me and a can of lactogen so we can have milk in our tea.

I am sure we are going to enjoy Pan Tsi-lu as he is an unusually charming young man and very intelligent. His father, who has recently died, was the Pan Da Jen of Aurel Stein's *Ruins of Desert Cathay* and for many years one of the most prominent officials of the province.

CHAPTER V. *Of a journey on horseback to Turfan, below sea level and full of ruined cities, where we were not a great success as archæologists but saw much of the busy life and trade of one of the most ancient of the cities of Turkestan, and picnicked in Grape Valley.*

DEAREST FAMILY,

W E are on our way to Turfan, on horseback, with Moses bringing up the rear with our belongings in a cart.

Turfan is one of the places in Turkestan that foreigners remember about, because it is below sea level and so hot the people have to live underground in the summer, and because it is dotted with strange ruined cities half buried in the sand where archæologists have found all sorts of interesting remains. But the Chinese know it for its grapes and because it grows American cotton, the best in Sinkiang.

We have beautiful ponies. Mine is a big black Ili gelding which we bought just before we left Urumchi. We couldn't find the pony we wanted for Owen, so Mr. Pan has loaned him one of his, a great red creature that arches his neck and steps out with much spirit but isn't as comfortable to ride as mine is.

We were in Urumchi two weeks, waiting for the governor's permission to start. I wish you could see the passport he has given us, a vast rice paper document with lines of characters framing a dreadful bearded photograph of Owen with a bovine-looking wife. Mr. Pan and Mr. Feltman, an agent of the Russo-Asiatic Bank who has been in Urumchi closing the bank's accounts, both wanted to come with us but neither could get permission, Pan because he is waiting for an appointment from the governor and must be on hand when the governor chooses to see him and Feltman because the governor lost a lot of money when the bank failed and seems to be holding him as a sort of hostage, still hoping to get his money back.

Feltman has finished his work here and wants to return to China but the governor won't let him stir out of Urumchi.

So on our way out of the city we stopped at the Russo Bank for coffee and commiserations and were presented with two precious tins of butter. Pan and Feltman rode out into the country with us till it was hot noon and after they turned back we cantered happily over a wide rolling red and yellow land with Bogdo Shan, the Holy Mountains, glittering on our left with snow.

At the first little inn we waited for our cart. We waited and we waited; and when it finally crawled up Moses reported that the cart was all right and the horses were all right but that the exceedingly ancient Chanto driver just dozed all day instead of driving them. He had a long white beard and looked like Father Time. Owen tried reasoning with him but it rolled off like water since he could understand only about one word in ten and knew only two sentences of Chinese with which to reply. He was evidently used to driving freight and taking fourteen hours to a stage, and we didn't fancy waiting until after dark each night to make our camp. It was too late that day to finish the stage so we pitched our tent in a meadow by the inn and Moses volunteered to trudge back to town to see what he could do about finding a carter who could stay awake.

Early next morning we were wakened by a clatter and looked out of the tent to see Moses back already with another cart. He had reached the city at midnight, after encounters with numerous dogs, the first of which he had been sure were wolves. So he said to them, "Don't eat me now because I haven't arrived yet." Then when he reached the city he was stopped by some suspicious policemen. Urumchi policemen are Chantos, the advantage of that being that if they arrest or beat up the wrong Chinese because they don't understand what he says no one can blame them. But Moses cheerfully told them he was from the *yamen,* and they understood *"yamen"* and let him go.

He dug the inn manager from whom we'd hired the cart out of bed and complained so effectively that within two hours he was on his way back in another cart and one of the managers with him. Father Time blinked and grumbled mildly while we emptied his cart of our lares and penates. I am sure he was good and honest, whereas the new carter looks like a double-dyed villain, but at least he makes his cart go.

That day we traveled forty miles through the wide desert valley beneath the Holy Mountains. We passed several blue lakes rimmed with beaches white with alkali and finally at dusk reached a tiny inn above a lake where we drank tea by the stove and waited for the cart to arrive. This had been my first full day on horseback and I was so weary at the end of it that I could scarcely stumble out when the tent was pitched to help with the unpacking. Moses got milk and bread and firewood from the inn and we built a fire in the tent, made much tomato soup for supper and tumbled into bed.

Yesterday we went only forty li and reached Dawancheng soon after ten. There were three big wagons in the inn yard piled high with boxes wrapped in felts and canopied with matting, and in the little caves left between the flat tops of the boxes and the arched roof of the canopy two families of Russian Tatars had made nests lined with scarlet felts in which they traveled like gypsies. They looked like gypsies, too, with the women in red kerchiefs, black bodices and full blue cotton skirts. They were traveling by night and at sunset time we watched the men harness five ponies to each cart and lurch out of the inn yard with much shouting and cracking of whips.

In the afternoon Owen's pony was shod by the village blacksmith and we were sure he was going to murder the blacksmith and all his neighbors before the performance was over. They roped him up in a sort of stock with two feet off the ground, where struggle as he might he could scarcely move at all. He was snorting mad at the whole business, champed around the inn stable the rest of the day and had a fight with my pony in the night which broke both their halters.

Today we cross a pass in the mountains. We have tied our ponies to a very green willow tree at the edge of an apricot orchard and are lolling by the brook to wait for the cart and enjoy the blossoms before we start to climb.

Turfan

April 27

I wonder if ever again in our lives we will live so perfectly or be so free and happy.

Sunday we rode all day through a winding canyon, splashing back and forth across the clear stream and filing along the side of a rocky cliff above the shiny new green of spring trees by the river.

Turkestan Reunion

For all of Monday we trotted across a windy, hot gray gravel desert toward bare red hills called Fire Mountains. The glare screwed up our eyes and scorched our noses, but the ponies were strong beneath us and when they scented water before we could see the tiny oasis hidden in a dip in the desert they cantered like mad till they reached the spring in a clump of elms set surprisingly in the midst of barrenness. We fought with them to keep them from drinking till they had cooled a bit, and we bathed in the stream and sunk our toes into the cool mud and slept in the shade.

Tuesday we crawled out at midnight, gulped tea and saddled by a guttering candle and rode blindly into the darkness for the thirty miles to Turfan before the heat of day; first through a desert of weird clay with ghostly shapes looming out of the dark to frighten the ponies, then in the light of a tired old moon the clay formations growing into great buttresses and forts and walled cities beneath which we rode trembling, and after that the horses sniffing and running at the fresh damp smell of a new oasis and this time a tumbling river and tall poplars and a climb up a high embankment to dawn over more desert. And at sunrise we rode past domed clay tombs and an encamped caravan and irrigated fields into the picture book streets of the Turki city of Turfan. It is a blissful wandering life and full of beauty and elemental joys and we are greedily wishing it could last forever.

Turkestan Reunion

It is already stifling hot here. We have come down suddenly from Urumchi on a high plateau to a depression below the level of the sea. Even now the streets are roofed with matting, and vines and trees are trained to grow over them for shade. They are clean, too, and sprinkled wet for coolness, so that there is a surprising difference between the temperature of the shady city streets and the desert just outside the city walls. They are brilliant with color and riding into them yesterday I was ecstatic. They are lined with shops hung with gay wares, brightly woven rugs and saddle bags and long festoons of red and yellow cotton cloth and counters of dried apricots and raisins and nuts and red pepper all laid out in neat piles. Unlike Urumchi the effect is completely Turki rather than Chinese. Many of the houses have carved balconies, domes rise above the flat roofs, and through arched gateways are glimpses of the wide pillared verandahs of mosques where five times a day white-turbaned figures kneel to pray.

The women and girls wear blatantly gorgeous clothes, a sort of Mother Hubbard gown of bright figured cotton or silk, black braided jackets, and kerchiefs or caps on their heads. The little girls are most picturesque of all in their bright quaint long skirts just like their mothers, and little embroidered caps. They wear their hair in two long braids over their shoulders and often paint their cheeks and eyebrows, both they and the women frequently connecting their eyebrows by a streak of black paint which has a rather striking effect. The men are impressive in long striped coats and white turbans or little embroidered skull caps.

We are living on the floor in an arch-windowed room of a big Chanto inn, and even now in April we must keep the room dark and sprinkle the mud floor for coolness.

Urumchi

May 7

We are back in spring again. But before I start on Urumchi I must tell you the rest of Turfan.

During our first day there we received calls from an official from the *hsien yamen,* from a young Chinese who wanted to sell us a horse and from a Tatar gentleman whom Owen had met in Urumchi, some sort of an agent of the governor who happened to be in Turfan on business, and who took it upon himself to be our host, found us our cool room to live in and invited us to an all day picnic at Grape Valley.

But before I tell you about the picnic I must tell you how our attempts at amateur archæology were blighted in the bud. One of the reasons we wanted to come to Turfan was to see the ruins of the mediæval Buddhist cities in which several archæologists have grubbed with much pleasure. Several hundred years ago this area was much more fertile than it is at present and much of what is now desert was cultivated land and dotted with prosperous cities. When the water supply began to diminish it was probably the Mongols in the hills who first felt the pinch. They would therefore raid the plains and gradually drive out the settled population, and when the plains became too dry they too had to move off. This was in the seventeenth and early eighteenth centuries, and it was not until nearly a hundred years later when the use of *kariz*, wells connected by underground tunnels, was introduced to supply water for irrigation that the country began gradually to be repopulated.

During the prosperous period of the Middle Ages all sorts of people had poured into this region, Uigurs, Turks, Nestorian Christians and settlers from India, Persia, China and Tibet, so that the drying up of the water supply and the consequent moving off of the settled populations left many empty cities to ruin in the sands, whose disgorged rubbish heaps are now delighting archæologists.

The largest of these ruined cities are over a day's journey from the city of Turfan and we blithely planned to set out for the one which sounded from the accounts of Aurel Stein and Huntington to be most entrancingly full of the remnants of palaces and lamaseries and frescoed cave chapels and most stirringly suggestive of the glories of the past.

"We want to go to a ruined city," we told our host.

"But the ruined cities," he replied, "are many miles away."

"But we have good horses."

"But this is April. No one crosses the sand deserts in April." And it seems that no one did, for April is the month of sand storms in the deserts and to set out for even a day or two was considered folly. So when we heard this our ardor flagged. Why should we risk being buried in a sand storm for the sake of seeing a few old ruins? We decided to confine our attention to the smaller ruins near the city and on our road back to Urumchi and spend the next few days photographing the "modern" Turfan, the like of which we had never seen before, and picnicking in Grape Valley. We rode one evening to see a ruined village a few miles from the city with remnants of a wall and towers and houses but nothing suggestive of grandeur, and at Grape Valley we saw some remains of cave chapels in the cliffs, but it wasn't until we were leaving Turfan that we were really stirred by ruins, and that was quite by accident.

Eight or ten miles out of the city we were taking a short cut across a sandy pass in the hills in order to see remnants of some cave chapels in a cliff we had seen from the road, and there we met an old man on a pony. "Aha,

foreigners," said he. "There were foreigners here a few
years ago digging in the ruins at Yar. Is that where you
have been?"

"No," said Owen. "Where is that?"

"Oh, just five li up that way," he said, pointing up the
valley we had just crossed.

"Let's go," said Owen, and we turned our ponies
around. "Mad foreigners," thought the old man. It will
soon be dark and cold and they will be lost, and he stood
at the crest of the sandy pass with a worried look on his
old face, watching us as long as we remained in sight.

Twenty minutes up the pleasant valley oasis brought
us at sunset to the ruined city. It was on a hill, strange
remnants of a high wall and turreted gates, of streets and
towers and houses, distorted by hundreds of years of wind
and weather into fantastic shapes and ghostly pinnacles
of yellow clay. We rode up into the midst of that weird
dead city as the sunset turned it a golden salmon pink,
and even though we couldn't dig for relics in its buried
rubbish heaps we were possessed by the eerie ghosts of
its dead past and knew its grandeur.

And when we turned to go, there was our old man
of the sandy pass, for the responsibility of diverting us
from our road at dusk had weighed upon him so that he
had come all that way back to see that we weren't lost.

Although our self-appointed host wouldn't take us to
a ruined city he did take us to see the American cotton,

of which he seemed more proud. I am afraid we weren't very much interested. It seemed an anachronism in that mediæval town.

And now for Grape Valley, the pride of modern Turfan. The picnic was a marvel. The valley is six or seven miles from the city and boasted of for its beauty as well as for its production of many of the grapes that make the famous Turfan raisins.

Our Tatar called for us at eight in the morning. We rode to the valley in a jogging Peking cart across a strip of desert and up a gravelly stream lined with green willows and a long quaint village of tiny houses and wide grape arbors. Across the stream we stopped at a sweet spot where bright rugs were spread under an immense grape vine which they told us was over a hundred years old and which formed a cool shady arbor. Beside the arbor ran a clear stream lined with fruit trees and under the trees was a rude open-air kitchen where food was being prepared.

Other guests had arrived, two Tatars in Russian blouses and two huge Chantos in skull caps and loose white coats. One of the latter delighted us particularly, a fat fellow who looked like a perspiring egg with a little black skull cap on one side of his small end and his clothes hanging on him like Humpty Dumpty and always coming unbuttoned. He was avid for information of the world and spent the day mopping his face and plying Owen with questions. In fact they all sat around all day on the gay rugs and asked Owen questions as if he were an oracle, one of the best of which was, "If sheep in one part of the world make the same kinds of noises as sheep in any other part of the world, why is it that men don't talk the same all over the world?" They asked about our marriage customs and how much Owen had paid for me. They were very curious about me as no white woman had been before to Turfan.

Almost as soon as we arrived a tablecloth was spread on the rugs and a samovar was brought and plates of nuts and raisins and big rounds of Chanto bread. The rugs, by the way, were lovely and we especially admired two big woven ones with a design rather like an American Indian pattern and colors which were soft and pleasing compared to the harsh aniline dyed rug from Khotan which was next to them. They told us they came from Lop Nor and that we could buy some in Turfan, but when we went the next day to' look for them there were none to be had.

After we had eaten all the nuts and raisins we could hold three big round platters were brought in full of bits of fat mutton which had been roasted on skewers over an open fire. These we ate with our fingers and a towel several yards long was stretched around the circle in the laps of the guests so that we could each wipe our fingers on our piece of it between bites. After these *kabobs* it was suggested that we climb up onto the cliff to get a view of the valley and see the little latticed houses in which the raisins are hung to dry in the wind. And when we returned there were more platters of mutton, this time boiled, and also eaten with the fingers, and tea again. Then there was another walk to see the ruined cave chapels with remnants of fresco still left on their ceilings, and when we returned there was food again, this time the rice fried with mutton fat and bits of carrot which the Chantos call *pilau* and the Chinese *chua fan* (grab rice) because the Chantos eat this also with their fingers, a very greasy performance.

We drove home in the carts at sunset time, the little Chanto drivers racing with each other over the rocky desert till we were jolted quite to jelly.

Our other days in Turfan were spent mostly in taking pictures and eating melons. Taking pictures we found very difficult as the attractions of the foreign woman and the cameras, neither of which most of the people had ever seen before, collected such immense crowds that we could scarcely move and quite obliterated anything we might want to photograph. The crowd was friendly enough and we couldn't really mind them, but being a continuous circus procession got a bit wearying and we finally couldn't leave the inn at all except on horseback.

But the melon eating wasn't so difficult. Delicious musk melons almost as large as watermelons are grown in Turfan and kept all winter in cellars so that even in April they could be had for forty tael cents (eight cents gold) apiece. They also dry a great quantity of them in the autumn simply by cutting them in strips and setting them in the sun. There can't be many places in the world where melons would dry in the sun before they rotted.

The night we left Turfan, after we had seen the ruined city, we were lost in the desert. We had gone ahead of the cart in the dark and turned onto the wrong road and after discovering our mistake floundered about on shelves of weird white clay for an hour or more until we heard the "oha, oha, oha" of our carter's call and miraculously found him in the dark, after which we followed close behind him till we reached our inn, a little walled compound in the midst of barrenness where we dug half a dozen Chantos out of a mud room for us to sleep in and I tumbled into my blanket too sleepy for supper.

The next hot morning, across more desert, brought us to Toksun, the town where the road from Kashgar joins the road from Turfan. It was a repetition of the picturesqueness of Turfan on a smaller scale. "Here come the foreign photographers," people shouted as we rode up the main street. Our fame as photographers had spread mysteriously ahead of us.

"Come on, everybody, they are going out to take pictures," someone at the inn would shout, and a crowd would rush after us in a perfect panic of curiosity and delight.

Owen dismounted to photograph the quaint gate of a mosque and a mob collected by magic. Afterwards a Chanto boy followed us and asked Owen if we were "Americanskies." "Some Americanskies were here last year," he said, "and had dinner at our house. I made them a present of a melon and some fresh eggs and they gave me five taels. Americanskies are very good, and since I have eaten the food of Americanskies I am forever indebted to them all and would be very glad to serve you." We guessed that these affluent countrymen of ours were Mr. Morden and Mr. Clark of the American Museum of Natural History, as they are the only Americans who have been this way for years. It was surprising enough to meet anyone in Toksun who had even heard of America.

We asked the boy about the ruins we had heard were in the neighborhood and he offered to lead us to a ruined city half a mile away. It was a ruin all right, but not a very ancient one, a relic of the Mohammedan rebellion fifty years ago. It was a queer walled town half built up again, in the center of which was a mud-domed mosque and two delightful old *mullahs* who invited us into their cool dark little room lined with rugs and felts and cushions for a cup of tea.

The next day we traversed the desert of deserts. We set out from the little Chanto inn in the oasis beyond

Turkestan Reunion

Toksun where we had slept, in the just-before-dawn coolness of three in the morning, walking the ponies slowly
at first behind the cart till we were well in the gobi and
the pink dawn gave us light enough to trot ahead. Then
we swung along for hours and miles across a flat gray
gravel gobi, dim hills far away to either side, the sunrise
red at our right and a long white road ahead. For twenty
miles we met no one and there was no break in the flat
monotony of the desert save the occasional skeleton of a
camel or a donkey by the trail and a single heap of gravel
in the middle of the gray waste. We rode over to the heap
and found that it was gravel thrown up from a hole in
the earth so deep we couldn't see the bottom. It was evidently an old and unsuccessful attempt at a well, pathetically unsuccessful, since the road must be ghastly in the
summer sun and coming from the other direction slow
moving carts and caravans would have been all day without water when they reached that spot.

At 6:30 we reached the crest of a slight rise in the desert
and found a little mud-walled compound and a sweet
old man reading the Koran in the doorway of his little
hut. He told us that his place was known as "Big Water
Jar" because all the water he had was kept in a huge
earthenware jar. The water, and his fuel too, had to be
brought on donkeys from fifty li away. He had lived
there for thirty-five years and had known of many men
dying of thirst on that road and numberless animals. He

told us that the well that we had seen had been dug for 400 feet without sign of water and then had caved in.

Another fifteen miles across more desert under an increasingly hot sun brought us to "Little Grass Oasis," a deliciously green spot at the mouth of a canyon into red and yellow hills. We tied our ponies in the little inn yard full of big carts which we discovered belonged to some Russians traveling from Kashgar to Urumchi. The innkeeper was all in a flutter at having so many foreigners all at once. The Russian, an agent for a Tientsin firm, his wife and two small boys, had been on the road two months and had elaborately rigged their cart with windows and doors. They had with them a charming Armenian girl whose husband had ridden on ahead to Urumchi. They invited us to tea and stilted conversation in Russian and we liked them very much.

Outside the inn there was a little stream running through lush meadows covered with wild iris and dandelions and we dozed there in the grass till the cart came. That night a tremendous wind arose and when Moses came to waken us at three we feebly decided to wait until it had stopped. It was well we did, as it got worse instead of better and we would have had to turn back. All day we kept our little room closed as tightly as we could but even then there was an eighth of an inch of dust over everything and we choked and spat and buried our noses under the covers. When we did start the wind was still terrific and we had to fight our way against it up and up into the red and yellow hills. It seemed to exhilarate the ponies, who went gloriously up to the top and down a steep road on the other side of the range which joined the road we had come on from Urumchi at a little Chanto inn where we had stopped for lunch on the way to Turfan. We had lunch there again and the rest of the day took us through the pass to Dawancheng. This time, instead of winding along the bed of the stream all the way we left the cart to pursue its former course and climbed on the winter road which went right up over the mountains. On the steepest parts we had to lead our ponies and it was difficult to see how carts ever got over at all. It takes at least three horses for the smallest cart going up and there have been many accidents going down.

The rest of the way back to Urumchi we did in an easy two days, traveling the last forty miles to the city before eleven in the morning. We passed our Russian friends at the inn forty li from town where we had camped two weeks before, and from there we followed a group of Chanto travelers with brilliant striped saddle bags on their gaily caparisoned ponies over steep short cuts up and down hill into the city.

Home-coming to Urumchi was great fun, all the servants and young apprentices at our Chinese trading firm running out to greet us and hold our ponies and unload our saddle bags, our big cool room of the curtained *k'ang,* and the manager coming in to hear of our adventures and then Mr. Pan and endless cups of pale and fragrant tea.

CHAPTER VI. *Of Urumchi, the capital city, of how we were guests in a Chinese trading firm, of Turkestan ponies and how we bought some.*

DEAR MOTHER AND FATHER,

I SHOULD like to live in Urumchi. The capital of almost anywhere is interesting, I suppose, full of intrigue and electric with rumors and uneasy with uncertainty and spicy with stories below stairs of those currently in the seats of the mighty. And the capital of Chinese Turkestan is a delightful place, barbaric and civilized, mediæval and modern all at once. There is a wireless station but no newspapers, electric lights but no printing press, no railways, of course, but three motor cars. Though to be sure the motor cars, the only ones in the province, are all owned by the governor and only one of them works, a Packard twin six some ten years old which works only very spasmodically. The wireless works spasmodically, too, and usually only for the governor, and until this month the governor was the only one who had electric lights. Our trading firm installed some while we were at Turfan and is duly excited about it.

Much of our delight in Urumchi is in its long and checkered past, and I have been reading all the history

I can get hold of, which isn't much. It is stirring reading, as Northern Turkestan has been swept by the tides of one gorgeous bloody race after another of the peoples that have plundered and settled Central Asia.

It seems that little is known of the first of them but that the Huns swept through in the first and second centuries on their way from Mongolia to Europe. But its known history starts in the ninth century when the Uigurs migrated from Mongolia and set up a kingdom whose capital was Bishbaligh on the site of the present Urumchi. Then the pageant runs something like this:

In the twelfth century the Kara Kitai appeared from China and conquered the Uigurs, and somewhere along about then flourished the fabled empire of Prester John, king of the Nestorian Kirei.

In the thirteenth century the Mongols took possession under the glorious Jenghis Khan.

In the fifteenth century the Chinese conquered the Mongols.

In the seventeenth century the Mongols came back and a western tribe of them known as the Eleuths took possession of the land, which became known as Zungaria from the branch of the Eleuths called Zungars to which their ruler belonged.

The stormy rule of the Zungars was ended abruptly by the Manchus who appeared on the scene in 1750 and annihilated them all. Then they populated the land with

Solons, Sibos and T'ung-kans (Chinese Mohammedans) to which were gradually added colonists from the crowded provinces of China and a great collection of criminals and outlaws escaping the arm of the law.

After this nothing much happened till 1864 when the Mohammedans rose against their rulers. The T'ung-kans captured Urumchi and killed 130,000 Chinese. Many towns were destroyed and it was not until seventeen years later that the Chinese succeeded in finally crushing the revolt and establishing their territory north and south of the T'ien Shan as the Chinese province of Sinkiang.

There you have the history of Urumchi in a chocolate coat and a nut shell. And doesn't the sound of Bishbaligh and Prester John and Jenghis Khan and Uigurs and Mongols and Zungars make you think of wide lands, great herds of ponies, rich rugs, gay banners and brave warriors in lacquered armor! They are all still here, ends of them, and living the same life, though wars and conquests are on a petty scale and one sees the cold and privation, disease, misery, flies in the sour milk and hairs in the rancid butter that the historians have omitted for the grandeur.

One can understand a little of how difficult a province it is to rule when one realizes that it still contains flotsam and jetsam remnants of every variety of people who have passed through or conquered the land as well as the scamps and villains who have run away from Chinese law. It is too far from Peking to be much affected by Chinese governments and wars and the governor is a king and rules without interference.

I have the greatest respect for the governor, whose name is Yang Tseng-hsin. He is the type of ruthless official who invites undesirable subordinates to ceremonial feasts and has their heads chopped off at the table while the band plays in the courtyard; and his province, full of divergent tribes and elusive nomads and a generous sprinkling of outlaws and ragamuffins, is the only peaceful one in all China. With wars and political chaos in the lands all about him he naturally fears for his power and will allow no newspapers, railways or motor cars in the province, rigidly censors all mail and allows very few travelers, all of whom he arrests on the border until he is thoroughly assured of their harmlessness. He wants no more contact than necessary with the outer world and while he carries on trade more or less gingerly with both China and Russia he is careful not to become entangled politically with either of them. His success in managing to keep widely divergent races living peacefully together is in playing them off against each other and he does it very cleverly, though he attributes much of his success to his soothsayer brother and takes care to stand well with the gods, though even of them he stands in little awe. A few days ago he ordered the rain god to be taken from the temple and beaten because it had not rained.

Turkestan Reunion

He has a spoiled nine-year-old son who delights to use his influence with his father to terrorize officials and to take anything from anyone that suits his fancy. When the governor dines out he takes the brat along, and wise hosts remove everything movable from their rooms which they don't wish to present to his little lordship. But the child also has the habit of paying unexpected calls. On his last visit to one foreigner they say he went off with a box of chocolates, a valuable knife, and a patent bottle opener, all things, of course, that it is difficult to replace in a land where nothing is made and there is no freight or parcel post. He has atrocious manners, reprimands his father and officials at table, calls his teachers by their first names and treats them like servants. All of which is worse in a Chinese child who is expected to venerate his elders and teachers than it would be in a spoiled foreign child. But it all seems to amuse his father, who thinks him a "chip off the old block."

Isn't Urumchi a comical name? It comes from some Mongol or Turkish word. The Chinese name for Urumchi is "Tihwa," although it is usually called by the Chinese "Hung Miao-tze" (red temple, from an old temple on a hill outside the city) or "Hsin-chiang Sheng" (Sinkiang Province). It is said to have a population of 60,000, two-thirds of which are Chinese and one-quarter Chanto. This seems to leave a very small fraction for Sibos, Solons, Russians and so forth, but it may be right.

Turkestan Reunion

It would look like almost any Chinese city if it weren't for the people and the things for sale in the shops. Walls, gates, houses and temples look Chinese and there are lots of Chinese people, too, of course, but the streets swarm with Chantos and Kirghiz and Kazaks looking even gayer than they did in Chuguchak, and the shops are full of fascinating crude things, brightly woven saddle bags and rugs and blankets and coarse red and yellow cotton cloth, bridles and harness barbaric with pewter and enamel decorations, ropes and bags of brown and white wool woven like a coarse tweed, and earthenware dishes quite different from the peasant ware on the coast. There are bowls and teapots that I particularly like of a pale green with dark green splashy designs on them. Very little is made in the province and nothing of fine quality. A little silk is woven in the south, but it is of a coarse quality, and here they make only the coarsest cotton cloth and crude earthenware. Almost all other goods are brought from China or Russia, and there are many prosperous Chinese shops whose fronts are open to the muddy streets, whose long-gowned proprietors and clerks sit behind high black counters drinking tea and chattering about the price of things just as if they were at home, and whose shelves display a bewildering variety of straw hats, scented soaps, silk stockings, china bowls, enamel plates, aluminum pots, *Primus* stoves, Russian matches, Standard Oil candles and Ruby Queen cigarettes. And usually a few tins labeled "Juice Orange" containing a colorless pulp which tastes less like oranges than it does like the Chinese factory where they were tinned, a poisonous brand of tinned crab, a few bottles of Hennessy Three Star Brandy and an occasional one of spurious champagne.

The Chinese firm where we live does a thriving business importing goods from China and Russia to supply these little shops and they are lavish in their gifts to us of cigarettes and biscuits and lactogen which they are sure we must like in our tea. Owen can be doubly appreciative of these gifts of what they call "Tientsin goods," having traveled the long caravan road on which they come by camel from the coast.

It has been great fun being guests of a Chinese firm, though we are sometimes embarrassed by their attentions. The young apprentices are always buzzing in and out with tea or cakes or cigarettes and have never heard of the queer foreign custom of knocking on a door. And we have had a funny time about food. They were so worried about our having what we wanted to eat that we thought we would be less trouble to them if Moses bought and prepared our food, but Moses soon discovered that it was out of the question for him to buy anything. Whatever we wanted the cook would buy for us and Moses could prepare it. This put us in the embarrassing position of ordering from a host. And we afterwards discovered that the manager had wanted to hire a cook for us from the Russian concession but that Pan had told him that we wouldn't mind eating Chinese food. Their food is delicious, but they eat twice a day, in the middle of the morning and the middle of the afternoon, just when we like to be out.

Mr. Pan is one of the nicest Chinese I have known. We have gone riding with him nearly every day, and yesterday he took us on an all day picnic with some other Chinese people to a lovely little valley ten li or so from town, where we loafed all day in a pergola built out over a clear brook and ate Chanto food, *kabobs* and *pilau* and fruit and nuts and tea.

On our way back to the city he wanted us to go with him to a Russian wedding in the Russian concession outside the city. The Russian concession is amusing. It has not been in reality a concession since the Russian revolution but is still called that as all the Russians of Urumchi live there, both Red and White, and it is still the center of Russian trade. It is a long street cluttered with little Russian and Tatar shops with the tall gates of Russian business firms at intervals and the large grounds of the Soviet consulate and the burned-out shell of a huge and ugly building which once housed the Russo-Asiatic Bank. There are also cart and camel inns which harbor caravans from Siberia and China, and the streets swarm with orientals who are Russian subjects or who are there to do business with the Russians. In the late afternoons starched and beribboned Russian women lounge on benches in front of the shops or walk out for an airing, while the few really prosperous families dash by in carriages drawn by huge galloping horses, paying calls on each other.

Besides the Soviet community of consulate and business people there are many White Russians, "emigrants" they call themselves, a few of them connected with non-Russian business firms but most of them doing nothing but taking in each other's washing. The emigrants are divided into two distinct camps, those who call on the Soviet consul and those who do not.

We did call on the Soviet consul and enjoyed it very much. He is a simple, straightforward, intelligent sort of person, has seen service in the Russian Pamirs and is said to be unusually well informed on everything to do with Central Asia. We had tea from a huge samovar at the end of a long table surrounded by members of the consulate families only one of whom spoke English, a delightful old gentleman who wore a red flag in his buttonhole.

The consul was not at the wedding, which was a gala occasion. We found the house full of men in stiff ill-fitting clothes and flowers in their buttonholes and women fussing about in uncomfortable organdies, a long table laden with elaborate wedding cakes and a canopy over the court with tables set for many guests. The ceremony was not to be until seven o'clock, and we didn't think we would be able to stay for it as the city gates close at seven, and when they are closed the key is deposited in the governor's private apartments and it isn't opened for anyone. The host invited us to stay all night but we were in riding clothes and didn't think we ought to accept.

However, Fan Ta Jen accomplished the impossible and we did see the ceremony. Fan Ta Jen is the Minister of Foreign Affairs, who had called on us a few days before, and he was also a guest at the wedding. He is one of those elegant inscrutable Chinese with beautiful hands and a mask-like countenance. He is said to be very anti-foreign and we had been a little afraid of him. He was extremely gracious to us, however, and as he too wanted to see the ceremony he sent a messenger to the governor asking if the gates could be kept open till eight.

We all crowded into the hot stuffy little Russian church which was complete with altars and ikons and incense, tall candles and a priest with a long soft beard and gorgeous brocaded robe, and a really lovely choir, and the service might have been very impressive if the guests hadn't continually whispered and jostled and chatted and elbowed in and out as if they were at a circus. Even the bride and groom whispered to each other during most of the ceremony while golden crowns were being held over their heads or they were being led by the priest around and around the altar.

The bridegroom was old enough to be the bride's father and had children as old as she. Urumchi Russians seem to be noted for strange marriages and as they are all far from home and with little to do but get into mischief they do seem to get most amazingly entangled with each other's husbands and wives. There has been a lot of talk about marriage in Soviet Russia, but somebody should write a book about marriage among Russian emigrants. It would make far more scandalous reading, from tales I've heard of them in other places than Urumchi. Another recent Urumchi wedding was between a man of over seventy and a girl of twenty-one who had had two husbands before him. I have never in a few weeks heard so much gossip of domestic scandals.

After the ceremony Fan Ta Jen said we must hurry to get through the gate and invited me to accompany him in his grand carriage. You should have seen me riding along beside him with footmen fore and aft. It was quite a sensation to have the gate waiting open and a great crowd there to see what the occasion was and all the soldiers at the gate coming out to salute. Gate closing is taken more solemnly in Urumchi than any place I ever heard of. Even the Peking gates will be opened for a pass or a little persuasion.

Aside from the Russians the only Europeans in Urumchi are the commissioner of the Chinese post office, an Irishman, and his English wife, a Dutch Catholic priest who collects butterflies and two charming old Englishmen who are connected with the China Inland Mission. Mr. Hunter, the senior of the two, has been in Urumchi thirty-five years and still finds the people impervious to the gospel. He has collected a vast store of information about the province and is always delightful to talk with. His fellow worker has come recently from a large Christian community in Kansu to take the place of a man home on leave and finds Urumchi lonely. We have naturally seen a lot of them all, particularly the post-office people who have hospitably invited us to many a good English meal.

The Chinese post office has been very accommodating about crediting our money from Peking to Urumchi. There are no banks in the province so that if they hadn't done this for us we would have had to carry heavy sacks of silver and that is always hard on the nerves in this part of the world.

We have had great fun buying ponies. Sinkiang is known for good horses and fairly swarms with them. We were surprised to learn that although they are very plentiful they are considerably more expensive than in Peking. Everyone has stables and the Chinese ride a great deal as well as all the Chantos, Kirghiz and Mongols, whereas in Peking only the foreigners ride. On the road men seem to be judged more by the appearance of their horses than by their own appearance and when a man passes another on the road he almost invariably looks at the man's horse before he looks at the man.

The Chinese don't put much value on a horse unless he is an ambler, and a good ambler costs at the least 300 taels ($60), but ambling is an artificial gait with Mongol ponies and tires them quickly, so that we cared more about getting horses who had comfortable trots and were strong enough for long journeys. The horse Owen took to Chuguchak isn't strong enough and Mr. Pan has promised to sell him for us.

We didn't want to be fooled again, so looked at a lot and tried several before we bought. There are several famous breeds of ponies in Turkestan, all of them the kind that are known in Peking as "Mongol ponies." The principal ones are Barkul ponies, which are small and shaggy and apt to be bad-tempered, Karashar ponies who have lovely arched necks and are the favorites of Chinese officials, and Ili ponies which are large and strong and seem to me much handsomer.

We bought an Ili pony for me before we went to Turfan, a lovely black creature with a beautiful trot for which we paid 300 taels. Pan loaned Owen one to ride for the Turfan trip and said we might buy it if we liked it. But yesterday at the wedding Owen heard of a Badakshan stallion from Afghanistan which a Russian has just brought from Kashgar. The men brought it around this morning and Owen fell in love with it on the spot, so we are buying it for 500 taels. Badakshan horses are supposed to be very strong and are certainly more beautiful to look at than the local ponies, not so stocky and more sensitive and graceful. They are both lovely to ride and we are going to have good times with them. Mine came back from Turfan in better condition than when he started.

We are torn between loving Urumchi and wanting to be off again. This vagabond life is so beautifully simple. Instead of jobs, offices, newspapers, railways, clothes, calls, dinner parties, there are only ponies and the long road, Moses and his frying pan, paper taels to pay for bread and meat and onions, and all the world to wander in till all the tattered taels are gone. Some day soon we are setting out for Kulja and the Heavenly Mountains.

CHAPTER VII. *Of the North Road to Kulja, of Iskander and Meander, and of robbers who perch in the trees. Of sheep on moonlit deserts and strange shapes and shadows on rolling seas of sand.*

Kulja

May 28, 1927

DEAREST FAMILY,

WE set out from Urumchi when the moon was pale and young and slender and when we reached Kulja she was very old and tired, but never has a moon made desert sands more magic than this May moon in Chinese Turkestan.

The reason I know so much about the moon is that we traveled at night because of the heat, and deserts that in the daytime would have been long blistering scorching stretches of sand or gravel were eerie beautiful. Moonlight makes any desert glamorous.

I keep wanting to shout to you about how happy we are and to rave about the loveliness of Turkestan and the perfect joy of our days instead of making a sane attempt to describe them to you intelligently.

We reached Kulja yesterday, having been seventeen days on the road, the customary fifteen plus an extra day at Sairam Nor because it was so cool and beautiful, and another yesterday at Sui Ting to call on the Chen Shuai, the military governor of the mountain tribes, from whom we wished to get permission to camp and hunt in the T'ien Shan.

So much of the pleasure of traveling this way depends on the ponies keeping well and strong that we started out with them in fear and trembling, for we knew that this trip meant hot weather and harder going than the Turfan one, and after all we had bought Owen's Badakshan stallion knowing little more of him than that he was beauful. Also we had to be responsible for the care and feeding of them ourselves, about which Moses knew less than Owen, and I, if possible, less than Moses. But they have been beautiful darlings and have arrived quite as sleek and fat as when they started. We have much harder traveling ahead, so we are still holding our breath a bit, but we are learning a lot about the beasts and it is all such fun. I suppose I shouldn't say "we." Moses does all the heavy work and Owen is general director. Owen always saddles them himself, too, with much pleasure, and all the grooming they get we do ourselves with currycomb and broom.

We have named them Iskander and Meander, Iskander being Turki for Alexander, and Meander because my great black beast meanders off the road at every possible opportunity and when he is in the lead with no other horse to follow he has to be steered like an automobile. He is being broken of that bad habit but the name still clings. I am sorry to say that he is a coward, and stumbles rather badly, too, but he has beautiful paces and can go like the wind and he is so sleek and black that I am fond of him. Iskander is glorious, and behaves rather well for a stallion, though he got into one wild fracas on the way, hurling himself madly about an inn yard after a lively mare and biting every horse in sight including my poor Meander. After that we inquired cautiously for mares at every inn we came to and cooped our nuisance in the farthest corner of the stable.

We traveled from thirty to sixty miles a day, which is much more than horses at home could stand in this weather, and we could go so much faster than the cart that carried Moses and the luggage that when we reached the inn we would walk the ponies to cool them and Owen would buy and cut their hay and start their feeding and we would have a nap and sometimes supper before the cart arrived. I say supper, but oftener it was breakfast. The first half of the journey was across hot deserts and through scattered oases almost as hot, and we traveled as much as we could by night. The first six days were on the same road we had traveled from Chuguchak, and it looked very different indeed.

Persuading our carter to travel at night was quite a struggle. We were traveling together with two other carts. Carters go in groups this way if they can in order to help each other out in case of difficulties, as it is no fun being stuck with a broken-down cart in a waterless desert, and because, too, bandits are less likely to attack three carts than one. Our carter had had an encounter with bandits only last year and lost all three of his horses. There are several stages on this trip which are supposed to be through particularly bad bandit regions. The first of these are in wooded oases where the robbers have the pleasant habit of perching hidden in trees from which they hang down to beat the traveler over the head with a bludgeon. Only one of these stages we did in the dark, and while the carters begged us to stay near the carts, which we did without reluctance, we usually ventured far enough ahead of them to experience the creepy thrills of watching for highwaymen hanging from trees. Later we went through some hilly country close to the Siberian border which had been so infested with raiding bands of Kirghiz that special garrisons of soldiers had been stationed all along the road and we were given military escorts.

These Kirghiz live in Siberia and are Russian subjects so that it is easy for them to sally across the border to rob travelers in Turkestan and then fly back over the border hills where they are safe from pursuit. Last year the raids became so serious that a special military official was stationed at Ching Ho, the nearest large town, for the purpose of ridding the country of so bad a nuisance. This official called on us at the inn there, bringing with him a very small son and a child servant almost as small. I gave the young son some candy but when I tried to give the little servant boy some too, small son immediately took it from him and ate it up himself. Meanwhile his parent, a surprisingly able and intelligent man to find in so out of the way a spot, politely questioned Owen about his intents and purposes, wanting of course to know if we were up to mischief. He urged us to come to his *yamen* to see him but it was then too late, as we were leaving early the next morning.

It was this official who supplied us with our soldier escorts, a new one relieving his predecessor at each barracks, sometimes once and sometimes twice a day. We had to tip them all, and our tips were evidently considered highly satisfactory, as each garrison supplied us with its best man and its best horse. Once the best horse proved better than the best man and ran away with the poor chap. They have had some shaggy cavorting little beasts and the soldiers themselves were a much better lot than the wrecks we'd had from Chuguchak. They were Chantos, who are supposed to be the best soldiers in the province. One of them, a merry lad who loaned Owen his clumsy gun to shoot at an antelope, could scarcely ride because he had just been beaten for deserting. He had been conscripted for three years and when his time was up and he was about to go home the bandit suppression was instituted and he was reconscripted. He tried to go home anyway, and that's how he got his sore behind.

The hilly border country is perfect for bandits, being

full of little pockets from which escape is impossible. The new police have built watch towers on several strategic hilltops, and at the worst spot we stopped for breakfast at the most important of their garrisons. It was a small log fort surrounded by a wooden stockade like those of the early American settlers. We found half a dozen sloppy ragged soldiers still in their bunks from which they obligingly tumbled to build a fire and make us some tea. Their house looked surprisingly like a frontier woodsman's cabin at home, as it was built of wood instead of the usual mud, with wooden bunks, and guns and rough clothes hanging on the walls. Ten or twelve men were supposed to be stationed there but the others had recently deserted, and they apologized for being unable to supply us with two escorts instead of one, though I am sure I don't know what good even two would do if a dozen or twenty Kirghiz should attack us from the hills. Anyway we rode through the winding valleys warily, scanning the Siberian hilltops for signs of Kirghiz bonnets, but nothing happened at all.

On our third morning out from Urumchi we saw the greatest wonder of the province, an automobile. Of the three in Chinese Turkestan, all belonging to the governor, this was the one of them that works. We didn't see it in Urumchi. Streets are too narrow and gasoline too difficult to obtain for him to use it much. But on this occasion the Soviet consul, being mindful of the prestige of the U.S.S.R., had borrowed it to ride to Hsi Hu for some kind of a shindy to which the consul from Chuguchak was also coming. The ponies shied at so strange a sight, and the consul stopped the car to talk with us.

Just before we reached Hsi Hu we met them again on their way home, we having taken six days to travel the distance they did in one. We had stopped for breakfast at a little village tea house and were sitting at the long board table in front of the shop where travelers eat in the summer time, surrounded as usual by half the population come to stare at and discuss us, when suddenly a general shout went up of "Automobile coming!" Everyone rushed around calling out the other half of the population so that no one would miss the wonderful sight and they all stood in rows with their mouths open while it went whizzing past. Then followed a delightful discussion on the wonders of this devil machine. "How does it get across rivers?" asked one bumpkin. "The waters part before it," explained the graybeard who claimed to know most about automobiles.

That night and the next were much the same. We would ride for hours over strange moonlit deserts and then stop to wait for the carts, spreading a blanket and covering our heads with the mosquito net and trying to snooze, until the ponies would shy at some strange shadow and we would jump up to keep them from bolting into the night. We had one long wait while the carters doctored a sick pony that cried at the moon when the men held it to stick hot needles in all sorts of places they thought might cure it. Then we rode ahead till we came to a wrecky sagging little inn in the midst of nowhere and a hut across from its big gate, on the doorstep of which we sat to eat bread and cheese and radishes, holding the ponies, who were too frightened of the strange shapes and moon shadows to be tied. The inn dog barked at us till he was tired and then the carts came. The cart with the sick horse stayed at that poor inn where they said the water was too bad to drink and we rode thirty li ahead to another inn which was almost as poor but where high black hills loomed above, whose purple shadows warmed to plum red as dawn turned to sunrise, and we were loath to go to sleep, on a blanket in the yard, because of the beauty of them.

The next night was most wonderful of all, moonlight on rolling sands and high white dunes. They told us to keep close to the carts for there were spirits in that desert that lured travelers from the road so that they became lost in the sands. We left the inn with a Chanto in a quaint Russian cart who was conducting 2,800 sheep from Manass to Kulja to be exported to Russia. We soon caught up with the sheep, immense flocks of them swarming over the dunes and being herded along by shouting riders on nimble shaggy little ponies. There were several Chantos accompanying them on horseback and we rode with them ahead of the carts, threading our way through the sheep and then on over the wide empty dunes through sunset until dark. We had to plod very slowly through the deep sand, climbing to the top of one trackless hill to see spread before us seas and rolling seas of sand with strange shapes and shadows that made the spirit tale seem probable indeed.

At dark we saw ahead a fire in a hollow and shadowy figures moving about it and rode down to find a little camp of men sent ahead to prepare for the coming of the shepherds. There was an iron tripod over the fire and a kettle boiling, and we sat around it, holding our ponies, drinking tea made from bitter desert water and eating chunks of bread till our carts came ploughing through the sand. Then the moon rose and we filed on for hours across the sand to some high hills, fine haunt for bandits. A wind roared through the hills as we wound up into a high pass with the moonlight lighting weirdly its steep defiles. We had only one companion now as we had left the others by the desert fire. He led us off the road and up a thin white trail, evidently a short cut, which took us abruptly over the crest of the hills. As we came down onto the road again we saw shadows vaguely moving in the blackness at the bottom of the canyon below us. "There are men below," Owen said to our companion. "How many?" he asked quickly, thinking immediately as we had, what an excellent place it was for bandits and looking terrified. We soon saw that it was a single rider, and he, having had the same thought that we had, was making a wide detour to avoid us.

The road led down across a plain and into a leafy oasis. We crossed half a dozen shimmery streams, passed farms and a mill and two old temples and stumbled wearily into the main street of a large town quite sound asleep but for the dogs who barked at us excitedly as we passed. Fortunately our traveler knew where to find the inn and we tumbled onto their best *k'ang* and slept until the carts arrived at daylight.

The town was Ching Ho, the place where we found the nice military official. We went for a walk in the afternoon and explored a lovely old temple which had been quite grand in its time, the only really lovely temple we have seen in Sinkiang. There were remains of rather handsome gods and frescos and carved woodwork, and Owen thought it had probably been built, as had the rest of the city with its gates and *p'ailous,* to impress the Mongols in the neighborhood. It had fallen into tragic disrepair, though a Tientsin merchant had recently given a lot of money to have the walls repaired.

On our way home we heard someone calling after us and were caught up by a *yamen* runner who had been to the inn after our passports and had been looking for us. He invited us to go with him to the *yamen* and we paid a call there on the *hsien* magistrate who received us very graciously though we had on our most disreputable clothes and felt awkward in his civilized house.

We had hardly got back to the inn when the card of the same magistrate was brought to us and he drove into the yard in a Peking cart accompanied by a servant bringing us a gift of a live chicken, twenty eggs, a box of tea and some candy. We mustered as much hospitality as we could in the cluttered little inn room and managed to produce tea, some Russian biscuits given to us by Feltman when we left Urumchi, and brandy which had been a farewell gift from Fan Ta Jen, the Minister of Foreign Affairs.

Our next ride was a short one in the fresh early morning across open country covered with bushes of pink blossoms whose fragrance was intoxicating. Once three antelope crossed the road just in front of us. Owen wasn't carrying his gun and our soldier escort offered his, but it was a clumsy affair and by the time he had got the hang of it the antelope were far away. We reached Wu T'ai before breakfast. *Wu T'ai* means "five stages," it being five stages from Sui Ting, the next large town. It consists of nothing but two inns and a military barracks.

CHAPTER VIII. *Of forty inns and the lake where the weather is born. Of the Chen Shuai of Suiting and how we acquire a sword bearer.*

TURKESTAN inns are romantic and filthy. They are romantic because they have always been here, caravanseries strung along the ancient trade routes connecting China with the West. We have been traveling along the old Chinese Imperial Highroad which connects Peking with Kulja, two thousand miles away, and while there is nothing about it that looks either imperial or like a highroad, for it is a shockingly bad road, it is easy to people it with endless caravans that have borne the wealth of Cathay to the bazaars of the West for some two thousand years. It is still thronged with the same caravans of camels and donkeys and ponies, the same ox carts and horse carts, the same foot passengers with bundles over their shoulders.

Since leaving Chuguchak we must have slept at over forty different inns and they have all looked just alike, varying only in degrees of dirt and dilapidation, low buildings of yellow mud around a wide yard providing shelter for both men and beasts.

Turkestan Reunion

There are two kinds of inns on the North Road, Chinese inns and Chanto inns. In towns where there are both kinds the Chinese carters go to Chinese inns and the Chanto carters to Chanto inns and we have nothing whatever to say about it. The Chanto inns are usually cleaner but are apt to have only one common room where everyone sleeps, a wide low-ceilinged room with felts on the floor and *k'ang*. Our carters so far have been Chinese, so where there is a Chinese inn we have gone to it. They call them Tientsin inns, as most of them are run by Tientsin men and most Chinese travelers are from Tientsin or near it.

I always love arriving at an inn. Our soldiers ride up to the immense wooden barred gates and hammer loudly. The innkeeper rushes out to open them wide, surrounded by barking dogs and calling, "Ah, you have come!" in a loud voice. We ride in and dismount, the carts rattling in behind us, the carters shouting and cracking their long whips. No matter how wearily the cart ponies have plodded all day they always manage to enter an inn with much *éclat*.

Sometimes the inn yards are a bustle of carts, carters and travelers, at other times still and desolate, a tiny enclosure in the midst of a vast emptiness of desert. While our men look after the horses we inspect the rooms. On one side of the square are stables for the ponies and on the other side a row of little guest rooms all exactly alike. At the back of the square opposite the gate is usually what they call the *shang fang-tze* or "upper house," which is supposed to be the grandest place to stay. It has a little entrance hall with a room opening off each side. We usually had a look at the *shang fang-tze* first, but in many inns it is so little used that it has been turned into a chicken house or a place for storing grain or is too dilapidated to live in.

We pick the cleanest room and preferably one without a window, as it is cooler and more private. The innkeeper sweeps the refuse into a corner, and if he is impressed with our importance, can be prevailed upon to produce a clean matting or even a felt for the *k'ang*. The guest rooms are tiny cubicles more than half filled with a *k'ang* from which projects a small platform on which a fire can be built. The walls are a pleasant putty color and the low ceiling is beamed and thatched with twigs and reeds from which pend fingers, like stalactites, of dust and soot from generations of the fires of travelers. There is a smoke hole in the roof where birds fly in and out, and birds nesting up under the ceiling.

The first things unpacked are the teapot and tea and Moses goes out onto the street to buy boiling water. Nothing is more refreshing than hot Chinese tea. We drink bowl after bowl of it, sitting cross-legged on the *k'ang* while Moses unpacks, makes our beds and cooks our supper. Before supper we unsaddle the ponies and rub them down if they are wet. We watch the inn servant chop their hay, or sometimes even chop it ourselves, with a long crude knife attached at the end of the blade to a block of wood to form a lever. It is comfortable to hear the ponies munching in their stable as we eat our supper. Then we stroll about the village in the sunset.

At dark the inn servant comes in with a torch to light the tiny wick in a broken saucer of oil in a high niche in the wall, and we crawl into our sleeping bags. And after what seems like just a minute or two Moses will be tugging at my feet muttering, *"T'ai-t'ai, ch'i lai!"* (Madame, get up!) He soon discovered that it saved him no end of time and tugging to waken me first and leave me to deal with my sounder sleeping husband while he prepared the breakfast and packed for our start at dawn.

All this talk about inns was started by my remembering the Wu T'ai inn, which was unusually nice. It was a Chanto inn and clean and cool, the floor sprinkled and a lovely brown and tan felt on the *k'ang*. Inn rooms in winter are usually suffocating with smoke, but in the summer their mud walls and lack of windows make them cool as a cellar, especially if they are kept sprinkled with water. During the hottest days on the deserts we rode all night and stayed tight in the inns all day, not stirring out at all.

We reached Sze T'ai (Four Stages) in the rain and

rubbed the dripping ponies for half an hour so they wouldn't become chilled standing about in the cold after a long fast ride. Then Moses built a smoky fire in a very tiny room where we got ourselves dried out. At sunset the day cleared and Owen shot two antelope only a few hundred yards from the inn. Beyond the bandit hills were green rolling meadows spreading down to a breathlessly blue and beautiful lake, Sairam Nor, where the weather comes from. Winds start there and the Mongols and Kazaks blame it for the bad ones and praise it for the good. We were asked not to shoot near it for fear of starting rain. It is stormy there much of the time, but we were fortunate to come on it in brilliant sunshine when it was as blue as Crater Lake in Oregon, which is as blue as blue can be. We decided immediately to stay there an extra day, so bought eggs and tea at a little restaurant and went down on the beach for a nap.

The next day we climbed up along the lake shore to an old wall where the road leads through a picturesque fortified gate just at the edge of a bluff over the lake. It looked very ancient but Owen thinks it dates only to the Mohammedan rebellion fifty years ago. Much of the country we have been through is full of ruins of those wars. Anyway we sat under this wall and read, of all incongruities, Floyd Dell's *Love in Greenwich Village,* one of Mary's parting gifts, which sent me flying over half the world to the old house on Bedford Street, which always smelled of leaking gas jets and where I lived for a year with eight other penniless but happy young immortals of the kind Floyd Dell thinks live no more in Greenwich Village just because he has grown up and moved away.

Leaving Sairam Nor we had a glorious ride along its green turf meadows which so excited the ponies that they cantered like mad the whole length of the lake. Alas for them, at the end of their canter they had to climb steeply up into the Talki Pass and just at the start of the climb we struck a terrific whirl of wind and hail. At the top of the pass was a strange cairn with flags flying from it and men sheltering themselves from the storm under carts or bits of felts, and the flags and strange shapes in the hail almost terrified the ponies into stampeding over the cliff. We descended into the pass in a rain which added to the awesomeness of the high black forest-clad mountains through which it winds. The Chinese name for this pass is "Fruit Pass" because all along the bottom of it and up among the spruce trees are wild fruit trees, their shiny light green leaves making beautiful contrast to the black evergreens. There are lumbermen's huts all through the pass and a crude mill or two and all the way along the trail we saw men digging a kind of root which they told us they exported to the coast to be used for making a silky gloss on textiles. We couldn't make out just what it was but I suppose it explains sateen.

Turkestan Reunion

At noon we took shelter in a little inn all built of wood instead of mud. An obsequious old innkeeper built a fire for us and by avoiding the rain which kept driving through the smoke hole in the roof we got warm and dry before starting out again for a long afternoon down onto the plain, where a mare led Iskander a merry (pun not intended) song and dance for thirty li to a town inn where I broiled antelope steaks for supper and Owen bought some Chanto shoes.

The next noon brought us to Sui Ting, a good-sized town where one of the three Catholic missions in the province is located. The inn there was so filthy and hot and full of flies that we went immediately to call on the priest, hoping he would invite us to stay with him. Unfortunately he was out, and while he came over with a cordial invitation as soon as he found we had been there, by that time we were unpacked and settled and having put up our mosquito net over the k'ang to keep off the flies were feeling a bit more cheerful. We called on him later in the afternoon, however, and found him a gentle creature with none of the forcefulness of Father Hilbrunner. He did us a good turn by chancing to mention that the official from whom we must get passes for camping in the T'ien Shan had his yamen there in Sui Ting and not in Kulja as we had supposed. We would have gone off early the next morning none the wiser, but as it was we stayed to call on him and made all arrangements on the spot.

This official was the general in charge of all the Mongol and Kazak tribes in the mountains, and he had for that purpose the most impressive *yamen* we have seen in the province. It was in what they call the "New City," some eight miles from where we had stayed, and Father Golomb went with us the next morning to pay our call. We were received by the general's young adjutant, an attractive youth so direct and outspoken for a Chinese that we were not surprised to learn later that he was the son of Li Taoyin of Chuguchak. He took our passports in to the general and soon summoned us to the reception room where we found him waiting for us, old fashioned and very polite. His post is a particularly difficult one and he is said to have put down three incipient rebellions in the six years he has held it. His *yamen* and soldiers seem unusually well kept up and his reception room rather elegant in a stiff and ostentatious Chinese way. He promised us passes and an escort, which would be ready that afternoon. That meant that we must spend a night there. The general despatched messengers to prepare a place for us and by the time we had finished our visit the best room in the best inn had been made ready and we were escorted to it and attended diligently until our departure.

Our passports, large rice paper documents in Chinese, Mongol and Turki, arrived long before the day was over, and with them a most amazing individual who, it was explained to us, was to be our guide through the mountains. He was a short stocky Kazak with a weather-beaten face the color of his almost magenta red coat. And this astounding face contained but one eye, a large lumpy nose with a wart on it as large as the nose itself, and bunchy black side whiskers. In spite of his appalling appearance the thing one noticed first about him and which therefore should have been mentioned first, was that he carried a brass-hilted sword a good yard long, the immensity and grandeur of which quite dwarfed its bearer. It was too heavy for him to wear so he carried it in his arms like a baby. "Why does he carry the sword?" Owen asked. "So he can commandeer things," it was explained. "The Kazaks are not allowed to have swords, so if a man comes along with a sword it means that he is official and so can take anything he wants."

We couldn't help roaring with laughter when we found that this astonishing creature couldn't speak a word of anything but his native tongue, of which we knew nothing. Only his complete uselessness as a guide could rival his picturesqueness, though Owen suggested he would be worth taking along for his photographic value. We suggested to the soldier who brought him, however, that we would like someone who could speak Chinese and he soon returned with a Sibo who speaks Chinese, Mongol and Kazak. He was a tall spare pockmarked man who seems to take life earnestly and to be impressed with his own importance. He told us we must have the Kazak along, too, as no one can venture into the mountains without one.

CHAPTER IX. *Of Kulja, where we were feasted by the Russian aristocracy, the German clergy and Chinese officialdom, paid for theatricals and encountered a Mongol princess straight from Paris.*

Beyond Kulja

June 4, 1927

Dear Family,

O UR five days in Kulja were such an orgy of feasting that we are scarce alive to tell the tale. We had thought that three days there would be ample, but what with provincial Russian aristocrats keeping up face and middle class Germans being hospitable and Chinese officials doing us honor the only times we had in which to do anything for ourselves were before noons and we had a lot to do, arranging for pack transport for the T'ien Shan, laying in supplies, washing, repacking, and getting mail off.

Packing is getting to be a good deal of a bore. Besides the little that must be done every day on the road we have to repack all our bags and boxes every time we change transport. We are having new boxes made here, as our old camel boxes are too large for ponies. A camel can carry over 300 pounds and a pony only 180. One comfort is that we have managed to cast off a good many unnecessary possessions and acquired very few new ones, and the firm manager in Urumchi sent two big camel boxes of cold weather kit and supplies for the Himalayas by cart direct to Kashgar. So we shall need only five pack ponies instead of the seven camels Owen had across Mongolia and the sledge load I brought through Siberia. In Kulja we bought two beautiful pairs of saddle bags, a gay woven wool one and a white leather one appliquéd in black.

Each city we come to in Turkestan seems more gorgeous than the last. A long early morning ride from Sui Ting brought us to Kulja before the sun was too unbearably hot. Our ponies were fresh after their day's rest and seemed to know that they were at the end of their journey. They always know the smell of inns and are ready to break into a canter when food and water is just ahead, and they even seem to understand that coming into a big city means at least a few days' rest. So that even after thirty miles of a dull road we were feeling brisk and merry when we trotted into the bustling bazaars to inquire for the Russo-Asiatic Bank.

Feltman, of the bank in Urumchi, had arranged for us to stay with the Kulja manager, so we rode right to the bank premises, a most impressive place with large white houses in spacious shady grounds. In the largest of the houses we found the manager's wife, a plump rosy-cheeked matron in a heavily embroidered white dress. She spoke only Russian but invited us cordially into her cool clean drawing room, large and well furnished in

the Victorian manner with a profusion of doilies and
vases. Her husband, Mr. Dubina, soon came home, and
while he also spoke nothing but Russian we accomplished
wonders by means of signs and meager phrase book Russian and thought each other delightful. They were charming people, wholesome and civilized and intelligent, and
while it was annoying not to be able to talk with them
we all had lots of fun over our attempts at it. Owen is
really a genius at picking up the essentials of a language
in no time at all and by the time we had left he could
talk about as much as I could after all my lessons and
Siberian travels. It was the first time he had tried it, too,
as before with the Russians he had always been able to
use French or German or Chinese.

They have a very interesting household, Madame Dubina being the type of Russian matron who takes great
pride in her housekeeping. Her servants are Russians, a
cook who lives with his family in the huge kitchen, a
laundress who according to Russian custom takes all the
clothes to the baths to wash and brings them home to dry
and iron, and a coachman who lives with his family in a
little house by the stables. They have their own vege-
tables, milk, and butter and their food was delicious. We
especially loved their beautiful garden full of roses and
peonies and rows of poplar trees which seemed heavenly
after our hot dusty days on the road. There were half a
dozen other houses on the grounds and the whole place

looked more like Europe than anything we have seen in Sinkiang. Behind the houses were stables and beyond the stables a pond and a wide meadow of clover. Beyond the pond we found the most beautiful filly I have ever seen, tied to a tree. Owen was wild about her. She was crossed English and a breed from Russian Turkestan. Our ponies had a beautiful time in Kulja with a big stable to themselves and lots to eat and little to do. While we were in Kulja, by the way, we had a letter from Li Fu Kwan who had seen our ponies in Sui Ting, wanting to buy them both.

Kulja is very near the Siberian border, and in the days of the Empire the Russians must have lived there in the grand manner and done everything possible to impress the Chantos and Chinese. Russians seem to understand better how to live well in the Orient than the more Western nations do. They fraternize with the Chinese much more than we do and at the same time hold more of their respect, and while the Dubinas are among the very few White Russians we have met in Turkestan who have kept the respect of the Chinese through their adversity, the Soviet officials have the same faculty of getting along well that the imperialists used to have.

Kulja and much of the country around it belonged to Russia for a long time. The Russians occupied it at the time of the Yakub Beg rebellion in order to prevent the Mohammedan troubles from spreading among their own people and it was only by paying an indemnity of three million rubles that the Chinese were able to negotiate through their ambassador in Moscow for its return.

There are many Russians still in Kulja and quite a large Russian concession, but the Kulja that we liked best was the Chanto bazaars, the fruit and meat and vegetable markets, the stalls of fragrant hot circles of bread, and the long streets of little shops hung with the gayest of saddle bags and rugs and ropes and harness and long streamers of red and blue and yellow cotton cloth. We went out every day just to walk on the streets and stare, and we loved to watch the nomad Mongols and Kazaks who had come to the city on an annual, or more likely bi- or triennial shopping expedition, walking about and staring likewise. We all stared at each other with the greatest good feeling.

The first day we were there Owen went to call on the Chinese civil and military officials and the Catholic priest, collecting invitations from all of them to feasts on the three succeeding days. The day after that the Dubinas had one for us too, and among them all they nearly finished us.

The first celebration was at the *yamen* of the local governor and was very informal for a Chinese feast. We drove to the *yamen* in two carriages, I with Madame and Owen with Mr. Dubina, the coachmen leaning back on their boxes to hold in their pairs of champing horses who took us charging down the street. The Russian idea of swank seems to be to have very large carriage horses and drive them very fast so that everyone in the streets must scuttle as they approach.

There were a dozen guests at the feast, among them a most priceless and surprising young person. She looked as if she were just off the streets of Chinatown, a girl of twenty-odd in travel-worn foreign clothes. The governor introduced her as a Mongol princess who had just come from studying in Paris! If I have given you any feeling at all of the remoteness of Kulja you can understand how amazing it seemed to meet anyone who had just come from Paris. And a Mongol princess! It was wonderful. The governor seemed to treat her with a good deal of deference as a person of some position. He said she spoke French, so Owen prattled with her in French with asides to me in English. She told us she had lived in Peking most of her life and knew everyone there, and sure enough she did, at least all the men, and all the scandal.

After half an hour or more of talking French she looked at Owen impudently and remarked with a perfect American accent, "You speak French awfully well for an American." He could have killed her. For the rest of the meal we spoke American.

I remember then having heard Mitro speak of her family, though she herself had left for Paris just before I came to Peking. Her father had been quite a remarkable person, a prince of the Torguts, the Mongol tribe that emigrated to the Volga several centuries ago, stayed there a couple of generations and returned, forty or fifty thousand families strong, to settle in northern Turkestan. He was some sort of an emissary to the court of Peking and his wife and several children still live there though he himself was killed in the Outer Mongolia troubles of six years ago. His son, a foreign-educated youth, had been in the *corps des pages* at the court of the Czar but had returned to the family yurts near Hsi Hu, and his young sister was on her way to visit him before she returned to Peking. She said her mother didn't know she was here. She had come alone from Paris, traveling on the train to Tashkent and fifteen days by cart from Tashkent to Kulja. She intimated that her studies in Paris had not been very serious and said she was engaged to a Frenchman, though it seemed probable from her having come to Turkestan and from her conversation with the governor that pressure was being brought to bear on her to marry within her tribe. She said that the sons and daughters of the six princely Torgut families had always before married within those families but the only eligible bachelors now were half and twice her age respectively and she wasn't going to be let in for anything she didn't know about.

She had the old governor absolutely dizzy. He was the kind of old-fashioned Chinese who thinks that women should be neither seen nor heard. Her short hair and barbarous clothing horrified him and her brazen Western manners classed her with the most disreputable women of the street and yet her position demanded that he treat her with respect and deference. It was marvelous. And all the Torguts in the neighborhood were coming to pay her homage. They must have been even dizzier.

So that feast was spent eating a great deal of very bad food and prattling of Peking and the Torguts with the Princess. The next noon we went to the Catholic mission to dine with Father Hufnagel, a fat jovial Westphalian who has been to Chicago and thinks America is grand. His idea of hospitality is to serve an endless number of courses of very German food and to insist most persistently on everyone eating and drinking a great deal more than they can hold.

His other guests were the Dubinas, a wiry little Baltic doctor connected with the mission who jumped about like a jack-in-the-box, especially toward the end of the meal, and a dreadful Russian couple who run a tannery and look like two skinny old cart horses. She was all hung with dirty chiffon and gold jewelry and tried to embrace everybody after she had had about three glasses of wine. He just stoked in the food and drink and paid no attention to anyone. But the Dubinas acted civilized, and the merry priest waddled about the table piling food on everybody's plates. When we sat down the table was loaded with every possible kind of sausage and pickle and we reached for large slabs of bread with our forks and spread things on them all over our plates. We did this for about an hour and then came meat and potatoes, meat and cabbage, potatoes and meat, cabbage and meat, until almost dark. He had a huge sideboard covered with bottles of white wine of his own make and some fearful kind of homemade beer.

Mrs. Horse shrieked, *"Oi, oi, oi, oi, pater, pater, pater, pater,"* in a higher key every time Father Hufnagel filled her glass, and when she tried to throw her bony arms around Owen's neck he began frantically wiggling his ears at me, which means that he thinks it is time to go home. So as soon as was a little less than graceful after the blanc mange and coffee were served we tried to say good-by. This was a long process, as the Father felt that it was a reflection on his hospitality that we could leave without reeling. He told us reproachfully that when he was stationed in Kansu, American travelers had never tried to leave his house without falling off their horses and he couldn't bear to have the record broken.

On our way home in the carriages we were held up on the street by a mounted messenger who presented us with a large red document which proved to be an invitation to feast at the *hsien yamen* the next day. It turned out to be a very festive feast with lines of soldiers to receive us as we drove up to the *yamen* gates and pompous hosts who led us through courtyard after courtyard of the decrepit old palace till we came to a large garden, a great section of which had been fenced off and roofed over with matting and hung with flags and banners. It was full of tables laid for the feast and at one end an elaborately decorated stage had been erected on which a warrior play was already being presented with a great flourish of swords and banners and din of drums and cymbals.

All the official Chinese in town were at the tables drinking tea and munching watermelon seeds while they played ma jong with piles of tattered paper money at their elbows. Far at the back and fenced off from the rest of the party were their wives and children all in festive array and chattering volubly. Right up in the front at the center was a long table at which all the foreigners, men and women, and the most important Chinese were seated, the foreigners being us and the princess and the Russians from the Soviet consulate. The Russians were a strange collection and not nearly as attractive as the Red Russians in Urumchi, especially a sleuthful little bank manager who sat opposite us and spent most of his time cross-questioning Owen on why he was there.

Chanto servants kept our bowls filled with hot tea for an hour or two before the feast began, pouring what cold tea we hadn't drunk on the floor all around or drinking it themselves if they happened to be thirsty. As is customary at Chinese feasts, one of the hosts was told off to drink Owen under the table and as usual the joke was on him, as no amount of Chinese wine seems to affect Owen in the least, but his host disappeared early in the afternoon and was found later laid low in the grape arbor among the opium smokers.

The theatricals were kept up in continual din from noon till we left at seven. The acting was bad, and as we were directly under the stage the bang and clatter almost prevented our talking at all. And the catch about them was that they were paid for by the guests. Everyone the host could lay his hands on was asked to contribute ten taels. And besides this, one of the company kept circulating among the guests with a red document containing a list of plays the company were prepared to act, asking the guests to choose plays they would like to see. One of the hosts went with him to the table of foreigners, urging us to mention our preferences. I disclaimed sufficient knowledge, but Owen, just to be agreeable, suggested a play he liked. Later it was revealed to all gullible guests that they were expected to pay ten taels for each play that had been "ordered." So the party cost us twenty taels and the joke was that Owen, having changed into his feast clothes, had come with empty pockets. He explained this embarrassing circumstance to his host who accommodatingly sent a man around the next day to collect.

Turkestan Reunion

The Dubinas' feast was the most difficult of all, for while everything was done beautifully and the food was delicious, the guests arrived at noon and stayed till after nine and we were leaving in the morning. It was lots of fun, as the Dubinas and their house and the Russian guests who sang grand Russian songs and the officer of Anenkoff's army who sang amorously to me from across the room in words I couldn't understand, were all right out of the *Cherry Orchard,* and the priest and the doctor were right out of a funny paper. But eight hours of them was a bit thick.

The Father was over early the next morning with a gift of twenty bottles of wine, but our ponies were already so heavily loaded that we decided at the last minute to leave them with the Dubinas. He traveled with us the whole first stage and every time we passed the pack ponies we were terrified for fear he could see that we didn't have the wine with us. We stopped at his house on our way out of town and he had a whole meal ready for us which, since we had just finished a huge breakfast at the Dubinas, we couldn't eat a bite of. Then we had to stop at the tannery of Mr. and Mrs. Horse who tried to feed us another meal. We managed to get away from there with only tea and cakes and looking through a large pile of picture postcards, though Mrs. Horse was determined that we should spend the night.

From the mission to the tannery, about ten miles,

Turkestan Reunion

Father Hufnagel invited me to ride with him in his carriage. Foreigners in Sinkiang have so little else to think of that they develop the most abnormal penchant for suspecting everyone of being a spy, and the good Father was pining to collect some juicy bits of evidence on us that he could report back to the community. "Well," he said, "I suppose when you get back to America your husband will be able to tell all about Sinkiang and who is Red and who is White and what everyone thinks of the political situation." He was disappointed in not being able to get me to confide our mission, but just on a chance he thought he would tell me what he thought we ought to report, the gist of which was that all Chinese officials were secretly in sympathy if not actually in league with the Bolshevists and when the revolution broke in Sinkiang they would all be with the Russians. He also had a cock and bull story about how the governor was playing into the hands of the Reds, in exchange for which they had promised him safe conduct into Russia when the revolution broke, but that their real plan was to get him to the Russian border, rob him and send him back to his enemies.

Speaking of spies, I forgot to tell you that the Red bank manager, who is said to be their secret service agent, was so suspicious of us that he came to see us the next day. But the joke was that he landed right in the middle of the White party at the Dubinas and had no chance to ask us any questions though he stayed for hours in the hope that the other guests would go. The doctor kept patting him on the back and causing him great pain by singing the old Russian national anthem to him.

In the meantime our Sibo escort has helped us a lot in laying in supplies and arranging for transport. We have bought grain for the ponies and sacks of rice and flour for ourselves and the men. Madame Dubina's cook has made a large supply of rolls and rusks and we can get milk and mutton from the Kazaks, so that with the stores of *kuamien* (Chinese spaghetti) and *chiang* (a thick Chinese sauce of which we are very fond) that Moses always lays in for us, and our ample supply of tinned goods, and what game we can find, we ought to fare very well.

We have hired five pack ponies for a month from a Chanto who is sending fifty ponies to Kashgar this month on his own. Besides the five we are paying for he has sent two extra, one to carry grain and one with a tent for the men. So with our two ponies and the ponies of our two escorts we have a caravan of eleven. Bardolph, our one-eyed Kazak sword bearer, didn't show up the morning we left Sui Ting and Sibo had to spend the whole first night in Kulja looking for him. Nor did we see him again until we were ready to leave this morning.

We made a most impressive show of leaving the city. The local *yamens* had sent two extra escorts to accompany us the first stage, who cantered in front of us through the town with a great clatter. Then Mr. Horse and Father Hufnagel and Father Hufnagel's groom and the owner of the pack ponies all went with us for the first stage, too, so with Moses and the two pack pony men, and Sibo and Bardolph we were twelve men and seventeen horses. Our poor little pack ponies look heavily loaded so we are going to eat as fast as we can in order to lighten their burdens.

Our two pony men are comical big Chantos, and what with Bardolph the sword bearer and the righteous Sibo we are really a delightful caravan. I wish you could see Moses on a pony. His mountain of flesh perches up on top of two sacks of grain and a bed roll and quite dwarfs the poor little horse. It is his first experience at riding a horse and he jounces the reins up and down importantly and steers the little beast as if it were a row boat.

CHAPTER X. *Of how we traveled to the Heavenly Mountains with Fido and Sadie and their ponies, and partook of much mare's milk and mutton with the nomad Kazaks.*

The Tekkes Valley

In the Heavenly Mountains

June 15

DEAR MOTHER AND FATHER AND TIM,

W E have left behind the land of long dusty high roads and cool dirty little Chinese inns to wander with pack ponies through the T'ien Shan (Heavenly Mountains), where there are no Chinese and a few Chantos and a great many Kazaks and Mongols.

We have camped with Kazaks for the last four nights and are enchanted with them and their beautiful messy yurts, their fierce big dogs and their herds of fat shaggy ponies. The Kazaks in this neighborhood are Alban Kazaks who migrated from Russian Turkestan at the time of the Revolution and were given pasture rights by the Chinese authorities. When things settled down a bit in Russia they wanted to return to their old camping grounds but the Chinese, who wanted their taxes, would not allow it and there was quite a battle before the Albans decided that they really preferred Chinese to Russian Turkestan. They seem much more prosperous than the

Turkestan Reunion

Kirei Kazaks we saw on the road in March and are considered the fiercest and most troublesome of all the tribes.

I am writing this at a little leather tannery kept by a nice family of Chantos in the Tekkes Valley. We are spending two nights here as our pony men wanted to have a supply of bread made for the time we are in the hunting country.

Our pony men are two of the most delightful creatures you can imagine, great big simple good-natured fellows. One of them is so much like a nice faithful puppy dog that we call him Fido. The other is very nearly a half wit and is such a comic great beast that he has been christened "Sadie the Girl Gorilla." He will squat ridiculously at the door of our tent chattering and gesticulating like a great monkey and giggles delightedly every time we laugh at him. One of the funniest things I ever hope to see was the time he discovered that he could see himself in the lid of a tin box of ours and borrowed some scissors to trim his beard. He would cock his head on one side, twist his ugly mouth about with comic contortions and then suddenly stick out his round tongue at himself and burst into loud guffaws. Fido and Owen both have the knack of making themselves understood in a perfectly strange language and have wonderful long talks, but Sadie just sits by and giggles.

Sibo bullies Fido and Sadie so much that they are terrified of him and were afraid to ask him to tell us they wanted to stay here a day to make bread. Instead they tried to explain by signs and grunts to Moses, and Moses, who is good at reading signs, brought us the message.

Our Chanto hosts are charming. The son of the manager moved out to let us have his room, the nicest room in the house with heavy felts on the floor, a cotton printed dado tacked along the wall on two sides of the room, a large low table in the center and plenty of cushions to sit on. As soon as we arrived a samovar was brought with tea and delicious fresh bread, and soon all the men of the establishment, half a dozen fine-looking chaps, came in with an immense platter of *pilaf*. We all sat about the candlelit table eating great quantities and attempting to converse. Some of the Chantos know a little Chinese and Owen, who is picking up Chanto fast, learned from them the Chanto and Kazak names for all the animals in the mountains. Today it has been raining and we have loafed in the house writing letters and feasting on fresh bread and mutton.

The Chantos have presented us with a tame bird, a strange creature neither of us had ever seen before, about the size of a large hen. Owen said airily he thought it might be a ptarmigan but I don't think he has the faintest notion what a ptarmigan is. Anyway we christened it Jemima and it slept in our room last night, but it seems a little difficult to take it into the mountains so we have decided to leave it here until we are on our way back.

Turkestan Reunion

This is the second time this week we have stayed with Chantos. The first night after leaving Kulja was spent at one of the loveliest places we have seen before or since, a prosperous Chanto home in a little village with a wide cool clean verandah extending into the courtyard, the ceiling and eaves of carved wood and the floor covered with gaily colored felts and cushions in most attractive designs. The host spread bright silk quilts for us to lie on and brought a little low table on which we had our supper. A sheep was killed in our honor and boiled in a great iron kettle over a fire in the courtyard. When we went to sleep on the verandah the men were still sitting in the circle of yellow light it made in the night waiting for the mutton to be cooked.

We set out about eight the next morning, the owner of our pack ponies, who had come all the way from Kulja to see us off, riding out with us a mile or two to say good-by. In another hour or so we came to a little village where our Sibo escort suggested that we stop to have some tea. He took us into a Chanto house where there was a delightfully cool clean inner room lined as usual with bright felts and with some very attractive old Khotan rugs on the *k'ang*. At the back of the *k'ang,* in recesses in the putty-colored walls, were piles of gay silk quilts and cushions and quaint old lacquered boxes and chests, and suspended from pegs at intervals around the walls were long clean towels with bright striped borders.

Turkestan Reunion

The women in long loose white gowns poured water over our hands from a brass pitcher in true Mohammedan style and then brought a low table on which they piled rounds of bread, bowls of sour cream, boiled eggs and tea. We loafed there on the *k'ang* a couple of hours, and for the rest of the day wound our way slowly into the foothills.

That afternoon, in his attempt to find the camp of the Alban chieftain of the district where we could spend the night, Bardolph, our one-eyed sword bearer, succeeded in getting us thoroughly lost. We climbed over steep hills from one group of yurts to another, at one place skirting an almost perpendicular cliff where the ponies slipped in the loose gravel at almost every step, and we wondered how Moses, coming along behind with the pack ponies, would like his first day of horseback riding.

It was glorious country. Below the glittering snows of the Heavenly Mountains were ragged black forests of spruce, and below the forests were the greenest of green meadows gay with buttercups. Fingers of dark green forest reached down between the meadows, hiding mountain streams that tumbled through deep rocky gorges down through the foothills to the Ili River.

The white domed yurts which dotted the silky green upland downs, surrounded by herds of ponies and sheep and goats growing fat and frisky on the rich grass, made us modify our impressions of the harshness and rigor of nomad life which we had formed on the North Road in March when we met caravans moving slowly and painfully through the deep snow from camp to camp. These Kazaks of the T'ien Shan live in the winter in the protected fastnesses of the high mountains, in the spring and summer moving farther and farther down toward the plains as the upper pastures are exhausted. All of their life is conditioned by the welfare of their flocks, but in June that life is prosperous and easy.

At sunset we rode over the crest of a hill and looked down into a wide warm meadow where there was a cluster of white yurts, the chieftain's camp at last. As we zigzagged down the steep hillside the ewes were being brought in for the evening milking and tied in long rows on either side of a rope fastened at its ends to pegs in the ground. Just as we reached camp the milking was finished and the ewes were released to feed their lambs, stampeding and bleating in utter confusion as they nosed about among the excited hungry little roly-poly balls of wool on the green hillside trying to find their own babies.

The old chief came out to meet us and two younger men led our ponies to the door of the largest yurt, helped us to dismount, and held open the felt curtain of the door for us to enter. It was a beautiful yurt, a round domed room with colored felts on the floor, walls lined with a matting of wool-wrapped reeds, and with great arcs of woven woolen bands in geometric designs of dark reds and greens binding the square felts onto the framework which formed the domed roof. In the middle of the yurt floor was a fireplace, beyond which we were invited to sit on a felt in the place of honor, opposite the door. Behind us were piles of folded felts and colored blankets and all about the walls hung saddles and bridles trimmed with pewter or silver and enamel, leather bottles and bags and brass and pewter utensils of various sorts.

There were several large wooden bowls of milk on the ground near the door. The Kazaks live largely on milk, which they either eat as sour curds or boil in a large shallow iron cauldron to raise the cream which they dry into hard cakes. They use it, too, sweet or sour, in their tea, with which they sometimes eat small squares of bread, the flour for which is brought from Kulja. Only the poorer families who cannot make a living from their flocks will stoop to raise a little grain. They despise farming and do it badly.

The chief ordered a sheep killed in our honor, which was busily stewing when Moses and the pack ponies arrived an hour or two in our wake. The whole family moved out of the chieftain's yurt to leave it for us when we arrived, but we slept out of doors under a sky full of stars.

The next day was a long and beautiful ride through a fragrant canyon of black spruces which brought us out at more yurts on the far side of the first range of hills where once more they killed a sheep for us. Here all the neighbors came in to share the feast of mutton, the men sitting cross-legged about the fire, which glimmered strangely on their rugged brown faces and their dirty red and brown *kaftans* as they drank *kumiss* noisily from wooden bowls and attempted to make conversation with Owen through Sibo and Bardolph.

This was our first taste of *kumiss,* the "fermented milk of mares." It is very sour and a little furry and is said to be intoxicating, though we never saw anyone more than mildly cheerful from it. The Kazaks keep a continual supply in a colt skin hanging from the wall of the yurt, with a wooden stick, a sort of dasher, protruding from the neck with which the milk is stirred just before drinking.

In the meantime the women were preparing the feast. The sheep had been cut in pieces and boiled in a great shallow iron pot set over a fire in a hole in the ground in front of the yurt. When it was brought in our host and several other men gathered around to distribute it into half a dozen wooden plates and bowls, the choicest bits being set aside for us, the next for the chief men and so on. It took a great deal of discussion and sorting and resorting, so that each piece had been handled half a dozen times by as many men before it was allowed to remain on its plate. Water was poured over our hands. We dried them on a red cotton towel that looked as if it had seen a good many mutton feasts since it had seen a bath. Then the plates of meat were distributed, a group gathering about each plate, and we all set to with our fingers.

In the center of our plate was the head in a rather uncouth state, with singed hairs about the ears, and staring eyes. It is considered the greatest delicacy of all, but I must confess it rather wrecked my appetite. We had the brains, too, and the tongue and palate and a piece of the tail and other choice bits whose geography I couldn't recognize.

For the next few minutes everyone worked hard with a great noise of sucking and guzzling. Each bone was worked at, scraped and licked till no dog would any longer be interested in it, and then cracked for the marrow which was sucked out with much *éclat*. Everyone was much too busy to talk, and when the last bone was finished the water in which the sheep was cooked was passed around in bowls and, the sheep having been well fed on good green grass, it made a delicious soup.

The men wiped their greasy fingers on their high leather boots, and when everyone had finished they stroked their ragged beards in unison and gazed heavenward, muttering thanks to Allah.

The road to the next Kazak encampment led over open downs in the soft freshness of the early morning. It was that delicious time between spring and summer when the landscape looks like a Swiss advertisement for milk chocolate or a summer hotel, bright green grass, bright yellow buttercups, bright blue sky. We were passed by Kazaks galloping on ponies, tearing over the downs and then almost straight up a steep hillside to join men waiting at the top. Sibo said they were practising for a race. Then riderless horses came cantering with flying tails into a meadow at our right, followed by a mounted Kazak carrying a long pole with a loop of rope at the end of it with which he was trying to capture a horse, slipping it over his head like a lasso.

The encampment was large, ten or fifteen yurts, and evidently rich, as the women wore unusually grand headdresses and heavy silver rings and bracelets. Kazak women's headdresses are lovely, a sort of white bonnet fitting tightly over the head and around the face and coming down over the shoulders in a flaring cone, with a strip of embroidery, usually red cross-stitch, under the chin or in a band across the forehead. The young girls are bare-headed, with their hair in long plaits, and they have bright beads and buttons sewed in rows on the front of their bodices, and almost always a Russian silver coin or two. I wanted to buy some of their rings, heavy squares, ovals or octagons of silver with quaint designs traced on them, but they wouldn't give them up for anything but silver. We had only paper money with us, which meant nothing to them. Like the Mongols, silver is the only thing they really value, and they keep most of their wealth on their women in the shape of jewelry and decorations. They know nothing of the money value of most things, and a ten-cent pipe lighter or an old tin can seems to them a magnificent present, but only silver can buy silver.

CHAPTER XI. *Of how we cross a perilous ford and camp at a tannery. Of our opium-smoking Sibo and of how we begin to suspect that Kazak hospitality is merely the fruit of Chinese imperialism.*

WE spent a hazardous morning fording the Tekkes River. We had come at the worst time of year for rivers, which were at their highest from the melting snows, and the Tekkes was so high and swift that at the last two camps the graybeards had all said we couldn't get across and would either have to wait several weeks for the water to go down or make a detour of a week back to the main road from Kulja to the Muzart Pass, where there is a bridge. We sent scouts ahead, however, who returned to report that there were Kazaks camped with their families near the river, waiting for the water to go down, who had been back and forth across the ford a number of times assisting courageous travelers who didn't have babies and yurts to carry, and that they were willing to help us.

Owen and I rode ahead with the Sibo, and were looking doubtfully at the river, a raging torrent some two hundred yards across, when far off beyond an island and considerably to our left we saw black specks descending into the water. We watched them breathlessly as they zigzagged slowly toward us and became discernible as mounted men, and after what seemed like ages of battling against the current they scrambled up the bank just at our feet, the horses looking like drowned rats and the men soaked to the waist. They were two Chanto travelers being helped across by four or five Kazaks whom Sibo immediately enlisted to take Owen and me back with them.

We tied our saddle bags as high as possible onto our ponies' backs, took off our riding boots and tied them on top of the saddle bags, and were ready to start. The river was deep as well as swift and the bottom was very unevenly covered with large slippery rolling boulders, so that we could not have attempted to cross it alone, and even with Kazaks to help us who had crossed many times and knew the bottom and rode the most sure-footed ponies, it was exciting enough; for, if a horse once lost his footing on a slippery rock and fell, the swiftness of the current would prevent his ever getting on his feet again. In some places it seemed as if all the world were rushing past us at a dizzying rate and that we could be making no progress at all, and at one place the water was so deep that the ponies had to swim for a bit in the swift current. One Kazak led my pony and another came right after him, but even then he was terrified and slipped twice, once rather badly. After his bad slip the Kazak riding behind came alongside so I could hang onto his arm, and at last we got across quite safely.

We sat on the river bank and watched the pack ponies being brought over one by one. It was rather nerve-racking and we felt relieved every time a wet load was deposited beside us. Rushing water and balking ponies made the Kazak guides excited and hilarious and when they would start back after another load they loved to ride as near as possible to danger, whooping and shouting and lashing their ponies and then standing in a deep rushing current for us to take their pictures. One smarty lost his footing and came so near to a bad end that it sobered them all till the last load was over and Moses and Sibo brought up the rear, Moses riding postilion behind a Kazak, grinning and hanging on for dear life, and Sibo looking scared to death.

A few hours across country from the river brought us to the tannery, and now we are debating our next move, or rather trying to find out where Sibo thinks he is taking us, as we don't seem to have much say about it.

We are on our way from Kulja across the Muzart Pass to Aksu, but we thought it would be fun to wander about instead of going by the direct route, so we have planned to take a month for it instead of the necessary ten days. There are districts on this side of the mountains that are supposed to be a paradise for hunters and swarming with elk, ibex and roe deer, big horned sheep, foxes, wolves and bear, but, alas, June is the worst possible month for hunting. The skins are no good now and anyway most of the animals have been frightened far away by local hunters who swarm the forests in June and July after elk, whose horns are now in the velvet and therefore very valuable. Elk horn in the velvet are used for an expensive kind of Chinese medicine, and a pair were sold to a Chinese here a few days ago for 800 taels. Owen thinks that there is just a chance that we can get beyond the local hunters. But at least we'd like to see the country since we can't help being here in June.

There have been several Russians and Englishmen here, hunting in what is spoken of roughly as the Tekkes country or more specifically as the Koksu or Karagaitash. We had seen nothing more specific in books, no marking out of roads or stages. The Roosevelts were here last year but their book wasn't out when we left Peking. And Morden and Clark were here only last fall but we have no definite idea of their route. All of the foreigners who have been in this region have come up from India and into the mountains from the other side where they could get more information than we could, and better guides.

When we left Kulja we thought we knew enough. All these places were on our map. The Tekkes and Koksu are rivers and the Karagaitash a mountain. No roads to them were marked, but we always depend anyway on picking up road information from natives along the way, and the governor at Sui Ting had given us a guide. So when we were in Kulja and everyone asked us dubiously if we had a guide we said, oh, yes, we had a guide. In fact we are supposed to have two guides but Bardolph doesn't really count as he seems to do nothing but come along with his sword to commandeer.

It is beginning to dawn on us, however, that as a guide the Sibo is quite impossible. In Kulja he seemed efficient, but the second day out he got us lost, the third day he began to dawdle, and he has been dawdling ever since. It was on the third day that we discovered the cause of his dawdling. He is an opium smoker.

Now smoking opium may be merely a gentlemanly vice among officials, but in anyone on whom one must depend for steady travel, either carter or pony man or guide, it is disastrous. We had learned that to our sorrow in the grasslands beyond Kueihua. To an opium smoker his pipe is his master. It comes before everyone and everything and is so exacting a tyrant that a man with the habit is good for little else. And Sibo is being as bad as possible. He must linger over a pipe before he is able to start in the morning, he must rest along the way, and when the hunger is on him he wants to stop and camp even though he has done only half a stage. And when he wants a smoke and can't get it he is apt to be nasty and insolent. As a consequence he bullies Bardolph, he bullies our pony men and he bullies all the Kazaks along the way so that they are all terrified of him, and we can get little out of him.

We are particularly annoyed that we have been given an opium-smoking guide because we are so completely dependent on him. For the first time on our travels we know neither the road nor the language and as we want to go considerably off the beaten track where none of the Kazaks speak any Chinese, he has to do all our interpreting for us not only with our pony men who don't know the country either but with everyone along the way. And of course it is too late now to find anyone else so we are completely at his mercy.

We were told in Kulja that we would reach the Karagaitash in four or five days. We have been traveling five days now and seem to be no nearer it than we were before. When Owen questions Sibo about where we are going he always evades him. Either he doesn't know the country or he is trying to delay us as long as possible in the district where there are comfortable yurts in which he can smoke opium and stuff himself with cream and mutton instead of having to rough it in the forests.

Owen also tried to question the Chantos. "How far are we from the Koksu?" "Oh, one day or three or five. The Koksu is long."

"Where is the Karagaitash?"

"Oh, up the Koksu, three days or five, but anyway there is too much snow there now."

They are probably afraid we are after their precious elk. But we really don't care where we go, so it doesn't matter.

There is something else we are beginning to discover about our Sibo that is disturbing us more than his opium smoking, which is that he seems to have embarked us on a career of imperialism which we are perfectly helpless to stop. Our first night out of Kulja when we stayed at the Chanto house where they killed a sheep and treated us so royally, Owen, according to his custom, gave our host some money in the morning. Whereupon Sibo privately informed him that this was not to be done. "It is not the custom," said he. "These people do not pay taxes, and instead they are expected to entertain official travelers, so they will not understand it if you try to give them money." Aha, this is the renowned hospitality of Turkestan at last, thought we, for we had read in the books of other travelers how they had been lavishly entertained in villages and camps and how they were continually supplied with fresh transport and riding ponies and were never allowed to pay.

The next night at the chieftain's we were also supplied with bread, milk and mutton and when our box was smashed we weren't even allowed to pay for the one supplied by the Kazaks. The day after that the yurts were poor and still we weren't allowed to pay. However, we began to suspect that the hospitality was not quite voluntary when we heard that most of the neighbors had fled for fear our escorts would commandeer their horses. Every night a sheep is killed and all our followers live high and we are feeling less and less comfortable about it. In fact Sibo seems so enthralled with commandeering that at first he tried to stop us every couple of hours for tea or milk or mutton at a yurt. As a matter of fact we are usually too sleepy after we have made camp to wait for the mutton to be cooked, preferring a quick supper out of tins. But Sibo always insists it would be impolite of us not to eat some of every sheep and if we are asleep when it is ready at night he brings some in the morning, the truth doubtless being that he and Bardolph would have more difficulty commandeering mutton for themselves and so always say it is for us.

What is more, the dirty dogs are saving their own horses by commandeering horses from the Kazaks for every stage and sometimes they not only commandeer horses for themselves to ride but a man on a horse to come along to lead their own ponies for them.

With it all the Kazaks seem friendly to us. I suppose they are afraid to be anything else. Moses reports one man refusing to let Bardolph take a horse, whereupon Bardolph actually got his sword into action. He got the horse. We can't do anything about it except to slip the Kazaks little presents when Sibo isn't looking. It is probably quite useless to report his conduct to the authorities at Sui Ting, as it is likely that they encourage their Chinese soldiers to bully the Kazaks in order to keep them reminded of who their rulers are. So what we thought at first was Kazak hospitality seems turning out to be Chinese imperialism, and we are, so to speak, the goats. But at least other travelers seem to have been blinder goats than we and swallowed it all as some sort of personal tribute to their greatness.

CHAPTER XII. *Of how we follow up the Koksu to beyond the farthest yurts, where for a little while "the boss is not" and Sheepo foils us of good hunting.*

June, far up in the

Heavenly Mountains

DEAREST FAMILY,

TODAY for the first time I have
felt really far away. We are far away, of course, in the
middle of the mountains in the middle of Asia, nine days
by horseback from a town, over ranges and through
passes and across swift bridgeless rivers and then up and
up a swollen mountain torrent that bounds and plunges
along between beetling rocky cliffs. We have scrambled
up and down waterfalls and scaled cliffs and traveled
over high shaky log bridges and along narrow ledges
where I never thought a pony could go and where even
the Kazaks had to dismount and sidle along cautiously
for fear of being tumbled into the river far below.

We couldn't feel very far away when we were riding
into Kazak encampments every few hours and camping
with Kazaks every night, but now we are a day's journey beyond the farthest of them, two families who live
in lonely yurts on a ledge high over the river, and they
are nearly a day's journey beyond the next farthest yurts
in a meadow of buttercups where the women all came

out with wooden bowls of sour milk for us as we passed.

Owen shot an ibex and a roe deer at our two camps on the way up the gorge, which encouraged him to think that he might get a stag if we pushed on. So we left Moses with most of our luggage at the last yurts, as beyond that whatever we brought had to be carried by the men along some perilously narrow ledges where ponies couldn't venture loaded. We also left Sibo and Bardolph, as they were afraid to come any farther, and Sadie stayed to look after the ponies that were left behind so we have only Fido with us.

We brought Iskander and Meander and two pack ponies, though how they ever got here I am sure I don't know. We are camped on a ledge over the river across from gorgeous mountains where I can see ibex leaping about on the high cliffs this very minute.

But the main reason I feel far away is that Owen has gone off hunting and I don't know when he's coming back. He has taken a Kazak for a guide and they may be gone for two days and maybe more. So Fido and I are alone in this absolute stillness. Even Meander and Iskander are off having a feed around the next hill and Fido and I can't talk much. He brings me water and firewood and I do my own cooking and am having a heavenly time.

We set out from the tannery in a golden dawn. The ponies were feeling frisky after their rest and we cantered happily over high green downs. Far below us we could see the Koksu, a pale green ribbon winding between steep rocky cliffs of every vivid shade of red from a deep bordeaux to a flame orange. We wound down to lower meadows where there were yurts and Kazaks swarming out to the path to bring us wooden bowls of curds, and down again, this time tumbling and scrambling down the rocky bed of a waterfall. Here the path was so steep that we had to sit down and slide or scramble backwards on our hands and knees, and some way or other the ponies tumbled after us. The pack ponies had to be unloaded and the packs carried down by the men.

Below the waterfall we followed a narrow thread of a path along a steep rocky cliff above the raging torrent of the river where in many places a misstep of the pony would have meant a battered end. But the ponies weren't wanting battered ends any more than we were, and we went on and on and on, the valley, or rather gorge, of the river becoming steeper, narrower, and wilder in aspect very rapidly. The great rocky cliffs towered perpendicularly above us for several thousand feet, breaking occasionally into side gorges with tumbling streams and a tangle of spruce and underbrush. Ahead of us we could see a steep forested slope and beyond it a glittering snow peak.

Late in the afternoon we stopped in a little grove of trees and lush grass down by the river to camp for the night. This was the first time we had been able to stop away from yurts and it was great fun making our own clean camp and being free for once of a continual and curious audience. Wherever there are Kazaks it is necessary to camp with them, as they are all thieves and if we are not their guests they can consider us their fair prey. Living with them has of course been tremendously interesting, but here there were none, and beyond us there was only one small settlement, three or four yurts. They were too far away to reach that night but Bardolph rode on to tell them of our coming and to put us somewhat under their protection.

The next morning Owen went off early to see what he could see and came back with a baby ibex. He also brought the news, collected by Sibo at the yurts above us, that the road ahead was impassable for pack ponies and that there were several places where everything we took would have to be carried by men, over swaying bridges and around steep cliffs. We therefore decided that we would take one tent, a week's supply of rations and our bed rolls on two pack ponies and leave Moses with the rest of the luggage and one of the pony men at the last yurts. So I spent that day repacking and Owen went off again with the old Kazak from the yurts to see what else he could find.

I am afraid I am too domestic to make a really good exploreress, for I simply adore a day in camp all by myself and I always seem to spend it puttering around doing odd bits of mending and washing instead of writing letters or an article on the home life of the Kazaks or something equally profitable. I know you are all going to expect me to write a book about my adventures and I feel very futile about it. I have had letters from several editors and a "literary agent" expressing interest in my experiences as the "first white woman to travel overland from Peking to India" or the "first American woman in Turkestan," or some such and implying that the public wants thrills and that any account of my experiences exaggerated to the limit of credibility would be acceptable. Even if I wanted to exaggerate my adventures I'm sure I wouldn't know how. They all seem perfectly thrilling to me, but probably not the kind of thrills the public wants. We have neither been captured by bandits nor attacked by wild animals, but every day seems full of adventures and how can I tell anyone about them!

I can say: "We live in a squat ten-sided Mongol caravan tent, blue appliquéd with white scrolls. We sleep on the ground. We cook on an open fire. Our watches have long been out of commission. We have no sense of time and little sense of space. We go to bed at dark and rise at daybreak (usually). We take a week to cover ground a train or motor car could do in a day. We sit in a circle of leather-skinned nomads who never change their clothes and eat boiled mutton with our fingers while they crack and suck the bones with a truculent smack and wipe their greasy hands on their boots to make the leather softer."

But can this give you the least tiny feeling of a joy in life we'd never dreamed of? So much of the thrill is in the glory of the country, and the wonder of being here so far away from the world that people know, and of living this life of a forgotten past. It can't be told.

We have both been very well. Often at the end of a long stage my back aches with being so long in the saddle, and I am too weary to help make camp and sometimes quite cross. But it never lasts long. Of course there are other physical discomforts, too, and sometimes fears. I had a great fear the night of the day I have been writing about.

At sunset time I walked up the canyon to watch for Owen, but encountering an unpleasant field of nettles I climbed up above it onto a flat rock and watched the warm reflections of the sunset on the mountain sides, an indirect sunset for the sun itself had long ago sunk behind the steep high cliffs. I waited there in the stillness till the cliffs turned cold and I turned cold but there was no sign of the hunters and I thought they must have made some sort of detour and slid down to camp from the mountain side, for the Kazaks don't stay out after dark if they can help it. And so I hurried home while I could still see the path and found Moses by a roaring camp fire and supper ready but no sign of Owen.

Turkestan Reunion

It was nasty country to be out in after dark, and a bad thunder storm was blowing up. It grew darker and darker and windier and windier and then we heard someone coming up the path. I called out, but it was only our two pony men who had been up to the yurts. However, when they came into the circle of firelight I saw that they were very excited. They can talk only about six words of Chinese but they began wildly gesticulating at the cliffs across the river and shrieking *"Chang kuei-ti mei yu la"* again and again, which means something to the effect that "the boss is not," or "there is no boss," and then letting off a great string of Chanto. You can imagine that I began to have creepy sinky feelings. Moses tried questioning them and managed somehow to understand that the Kazak who had gone with Owen had just come back without him, reporting that Owen had gone down, somewhere, and that he had called and called and, searched and searched and had finally given him up and come home.

The next half hour was the most uncomfortable that I have ever spent. I knew Moses thought that Owen had fallen over a cliff, in which case there couldn't be much left of him. The Kazaks had sent out a search party. If they didn't find him soon I must do something. But what? My throat kept getting tighter and tighter and my heart churned and pounded sickeningly.

As I think of it now I can imagine no worse place in

the world to be left alone. It would be awkward for a woman to travel alone anywhere in Turkestan, and what a long sickening journey getting home would have been. But, at the time, the fear of his not coming back was so ghastly that I couldn't think at all about the future and only tried to force myself to think what to do next. And I knew that for a while there was nothing I could do but wait, which was the hardest of all.

At last there was a call in the dark and Owen flopped down by the fire. I laughed and cried while he told me what had happened. He had shot an ibex which had limped wounded over the crest of a hill and the Kazak wanted to go after it. Owen and the Kazak had misunderstood each other, Owen thinking the Kazak understood that he was going on home by himself and the Kazak thinking Owen would wait for him. He had scrambled painfully down a steep cliff to where he thought he could reach a log bridge across the river, but the cliff turned to a sheer wall of rock impossible to descend and there was nothing for it but to climb up again and go around a longer way. In the meantime the Kazak had returned and couldn't find him, had shouted and searched and waited and finally given up and gone home. Owen had had a hazardous and exhausting climb up the cliff, had had to carry his gun by a strap in his mouth to leave his hands free and lost his beautiful hunting knife over the edge. But at last he had found the bridge and stumbled home in the darkness.

The next morning we went on to the yurts, two lonely yurts on a grassy ledge over the river, and established Moses. It seemed amazing to find nomads up this wild gorge. They were poor Kazaks with few belongings, but what a time they must have had getting their yurts and babies down the waterfall.

Here Sibo and Bardolph struck. They insisted that it was impossible to travel any farther, the true and secret reason being that they couldn't bear the thought of getting beyond easy reach of mutton and mare's milk. Sibo's name has gradually developed into Sheepo, because of his penchant for mutton. Bardolph, on the other hand, simply can't live without mare's milk.

We routed them both out, however, and all the men of the camp, to help us over the worst parts of the road which lay just beyond their camp. At one spot the ledge was so narrow that even a Kazak couldn't stay mounted without being brushed off over the precipice and at another everything had to be carried little by little over a swaying log bridge with a raging torrent hundreds of feet below it.

A hunter who had come up from below to act as a guide for Owen came with us. The path was steep but not as bad as some we had traveled before. It led away from the river up over a shoulder of mountain and zigzagged abruptly down the other side back to the river again. Then around another corner we came upon some warm springs coming out of the cliff. On a narrow ledge just above them was a hut, a good deal of refuse, and signs of many ponies having been tied to trees. In the summer and fall when the river is low these springs are easier of access and many sick Kazaks make pilgrimages to bathe in their healing waters. An old Kazak was living in the hut and another in a big cave not far away. We camped a mile or so beyond them where the grass was better for the ponies and one of the Kazaks followed to welcome us with a skin of mare's milk which we drank beside our little stream.

This morning Owen and the hunter set out early, planning to be gone at least two days, as the forest is too far away to climb to by dawn when the animals leave their lairs. I am really enjoying being alone. And I even miss my husband with a sort of primitive pleasure, a sort of "my man has gone hunting and will come back with meat" feeling. This is the alonest place I have ever been and from the door of my blue tent I can see ibex scuttling over the cliff across the river and roe deer on another far off hill. The difficulties of the path we have come by seem to have cut us off from all the world, and I am very happy.

Turkestan Reunion

The next day

Last night in my solitary camp I was foolishly thinking about all the things that might happen to Owen
while he was off hunting this time when an objective
worry protruded itself to send subjective worries flying.

Fido had put rice on the fire for my supper and had
gone off around the next hill to bring the ponies home
from pasture. I heard him returning with the ponies. And
then I heard him calling me in consternation.

I rushed out to see Iskander, Owen's beautiful Badakshan stallion, staggering about, evidently in great agony,
and Fido trying to keep him from lying down. I know
little enough of ponies when they are well, and nothing
at all of them when they are sick, but Fido said over and
over again in a mixture of Chinese and Turki, "Eat bad,
drink bad. Nice horse very very bad," and I guessed he
was having colic. I was terrified and wished for Owen.
I knew that colic was very often fatal and I could see
that Fido was badly frightened. I stayed with them for
half an hour, patting Iskander and watching Fido mas-
sage his stomach. He broke out with little bumps all over
him like hives. Fido showed me how to rub them, and
when we rubbed them they mysteriously disappeared.
Then, suddenly, he started to crop a little grass.

At that minute we heard a halloo and around the jutting cliff came Owen and his hunter. He hadn't stayed very long after all. From that moment Iskander began to get better. But the rice was burned.

Owen was disgruntled. He had seen nothing but a wild boar, which he had missed. The hunter had been impossible, seeming bent to lead him away from any trace of game and refusing to stay out all night. This seemed to prove what he had been suspecting, that the Kazaks had no intention of letting him do any serious hunting in their forests at this time of year when elk horns are worth to them hundreds of dollars a pair, and there was nothing to do but to come back with him to camp. He had also learned from the hunter that the Karagaitash, toward which we thought we were moving, while farther up this same river, is quite inaccessible from here whereas there is a perfectly good and easy road which cuts across country to it from the tannery. All the good hunting is there and not in this direction at all. But we haven't time to go there now.

The hurry is that we have to get across the Karakoram before the passes close for the winter. If it weren't for that hanging over our heads it would be so blissfully easy to wander lazily through these heavenly mountains forever.

Meander and Iskander are getting fat on the rich grass of these mountain meadows, but poor Iskander leads a hard life. He was fairly tractable on the plains where there weren't many mares, but here the mountains are full of them. The Kazaks all breed horses, and just now the stallions and geldings are pasturing in the hills and most of the mares are kept at the yurts, so that he runs into them everywhere we stop. Also many of the horses our escorts have commandeered have been mares, so that he runs and snorts after them all day and it keeps him much too excited. He is always getting us into trouble. Next to the piracy of Sheepo, traveling with a stallion is the most unsocial thing we do.

I have never seen so many wild flowers as grow on these rocky hills. We're always wishing we were botanists or geologists or archæologists or anthropologists or something, but after all it is rather nice being purposeless and we fit much better into the landscape.

CHAPTER XIII. *Of the sad death of Iskander, of Ma Ta Jen and his Gift Horse, of how we gladly exchanged Sheepo and Bardolph for the Good Guide, met Sadie's wife, crossed the fearsome Muzart, encountered a madman, and were welcomed in Aksu by Postmaster Wang and the merchant.*

Aksu

July 4

DEAR FAMILY,

W E have come suddenly down into the desert from the delicious coolness of the Heavenly Mountains, and we are hotter in Aksu on the 4th of July than you are in Evanston.

The next two weeks are going to be a good deal hotter still, on the long desert road to Kashgar, but the last two have been gorgeous, the best we have had at all, except for a real tragedy at the foot of the Muzart Pass and an appalling day crossing the glaciers.

Of course for a week after leaving our Koksu camp we still had Sheepo to harass us, too, which he did increasingly, but everything else was being so perfect that we couldn't seem to take him very seriously. He kept on getting us lost and delaying us so that it took a week instead of an easy four days to get to the barracks at the foot of the Muzart where we could get rid of him. But they were beautiful days over green hills and meadows yellow with flowers and along the edge of black spruce forests.

Turkestan Reunion

The very day we left the Koksu we had gone only half a stage when we were met at a ford by two Kirghiz horsemen with a skin bottle of mare's milk, who greeted us and begged us to stop at their yurts for the night. We had no intention of stopping so soon, but the more we remonstrated the more insistent they became. As usual when he was needed, Sheepo wasn't there to interpret, so we affected not to understand at all, but just smiled sweetly and kept right on going. They followed us for about half a mile still talking loudly, and finally turned back.

We knew very well what had happened. Sheepo had ridden ahead to their yurts for a little refreshment, which proved to be so refreshing that he thought it would be nice if he didn't have to go any farther that day. He didn't dare to come out himself to ask us to stop, but he thought if he ordered the Kirghiz to stop us and they were insistent enough we wouldn't dare refuse them. We had gone about an hour beyond this before he caught up with us and announced that there was no water ahead. This seemed doubtful, so we told him to ride ahead and look for some.

About five we caught up to him at a clear stream where there was excellent grazing and a most remarkable waterfall dropping through a hole in an overhanging cliff into a great dark cave. It was a perfect camping ground, being near enough to yurts to afford protection for us and mutton for Sheepo and Bardolph, and far enough to afford us a little peace and privacy.

The next morning on a grassy trail we met a Russian who invited us to breakfast, at a settlement across the river. We had heard that several groups of Russian refugees had settled on farms in or near the Tekkes Valley, but this proved to be not a Russian farm but a Kirghiz settlement where there were several Russians working as servants.

A dapper little Kirghiz man in a semi-foreign suit invited us into his beautiful big yurt and introduced us to his mountainous Russian wife in trailing skirts and three shy fair-skinned children. He was not a Kazak but a proper Kirghiz of the tribe the Russians call Kara Kirghiz (black Kirghiz), and they themselves call Bölik Kirghiz, who had emigrated from Semirechensk in Russian Turkestan. He spoke fluent Russian and ran a little trading station, agency of a firm in Kulja. We sat on his thick felts at a low table while his wife served us a delicious breakfast of fresh bread and butter and honey.

Late one afternoon we camped at another small settlement of Bölik Kirghiz at the foot of a spruce forest. Owen went off with his gun and found the forest alive with roe deer, one of which he shot within sight of camp and within a few yards of Sadie and Fido gathering firewood.

Moses has become so expert a butcher that in almost no time at all we were sitting by our camp fire eating venison steak for supper. Sheepo and Bardolph had as usual disappeared. Moses, Sadie and Fido were merrily roasting *kabob* over a fire of their own. The heavy fragrance of the spruce forests mingled with the smell of roasting meat. The little brook sang at our feet and we were peacefully happy, never dreaming that tragedy could intrude on so idyllic a scene.

The harbinger of tragedy soon rode like a genie out of the darkness into the circle of our firelight. He was a most amazing little man, almost lost in a pair of long wide black velvet trousers, above which he wore a little black jacket and a white vest with black buttons up and down the front of it. He introduced himself as the brother of the Kirghiz who had entertained us a few days before, who had sent word ahead that we were coming, and he cordially invited us, in Russian, to have breakfast with him the next morning.

Accordingly, next morning we got the pack ponies off, Sheepo and Bardolph promptly disappearing after them. We saddled Meander and Iskander to take us down to breakfast, and as usual before starting, we took them to the brook for a drink. Meander would not drink, but Iskander drank a lot, and almost immediately began to blow up and stagger about with colic.

Our hearts sank. Our men had all gone, and we knew nothing at all about curing colic. There seemed to be nothing to do but to take him to the little Kirghiz. All

Kirghiz are horse doctors, and while they have some practices which seem to us cruel and needless they do effect many cures. Whether it is because of or in spite of their methods we couldn't tell, but our adored Iskander was in bad need of attention of some sort and we decided to take a chance on showing him to Velvet Trousers.

The little man was very businesslike and started to work immediately, strangling him with ropes and galloping him to make him break wind, cutting swellings out of his nostrils, and all manner of things, some of which looked pretty barbarous. Finally he stopped and mopped his brow and announced that Iskander would soon be all right but that we would have to stay over a day before riding him. He did seem lots better, and we began to breathe more freely.

This superior Kirghiz lived in a house, a very clean little two-room wooden house, and we were taken into the best room, lined with rugs and furnished with a bed piled to the ceiling with silk quilts, and served an excellent breakfast, bread and cream and tea and dried apricots. As the crown of the feast a bowl of butter was drawn out from under the bed and placed between the two of us.

After breakfast we went out to look at Iskander, and instead of finding him better we found him very much worse. All day long the little Kirghiz worked over him. We would watch him as long as we could stand it and then go in the house and sit on the floor and want to weep, and read aloud to each other instead. The woman had spread quilts on the floor for us to lie on, and the room was rather dark and we felt very funereal. We had grown to love Iskander, and by noon we realized that there was very little hope of his living. In the afternoon it rained. He had been lying half dead for a long time and suddenly before dark he rose and galloped gloriously off behind a hill and died like a warrior, alone. We wanted to die, too. In fact we were so sentimental about him that it was a long time before we realized that we had not only lost a friend but all the passage money home that we had invested in him so hopefully.

We began to think about that only when we had to face the question of how Owen was going to get to India without Iskander to ride, as well as how we were going to get home without the small fortune we were expecting to get from selling him in Kashgar.

No sooner had Iskander died than our host turned suddenly from horse doctor into horse dealer. He wanted to sell us another. He had a large selection of good horses for sale at any price we wished. We finally made him understand in our slender Russian that, as we had forwarded all our money to Aksu and Kashgar except a very little for use on the road, we didn't have any price at all. But he continued nobly hospitable to the end.

That night they killed a sheep to cheer us and we had

an elaborate mutton feast. If we had been feeling more cheerful we would have been more stirred, as it was grand, and the family truly delightful. This little Kirghiz also had a mountainous wife, and a sweet young daughter and a most adorable small son, aged three, who wore a sweeping feather in his little hat and a tiny bright red suit with bright brass buttons on it and infinitesimal high leather boots. He had for a pet a tiny baby deer that went hopping about on stiff long legs. They called it "English Horse" because its legs were so long and slender. There was also a brother and four or five servants and we all sat on the floor around a big red tablecloth. The mutton was brought in big platters. As usual we were given all the choice pieces. Then the two brothers had what they wanted. What they didn't want they gave to the women and what the women didn't want they handed to the servants who sat by the door. Our host made a little bowl of sauce of the soup and salt and pepper in which we dipped our bits of meat. He was quite evidently delighted when we didn't eat all the head but left some bits of it for him. Then we had the soup with noodles in it and went very full to bed.

The next morning a Kazak from the yurts where Sheepo and our luggage had spent the night came to see what had happened to us, and after breakfast we set off with him, Owen on a horse borrowed from Velvet Trousers. I gave his wife a turquoise ring, but had no sooner turned my back than her lordly husband appropriated it for himself. He rode part way with us to some yurts where we drank mare's milk and changed the pony he had loaned Owen for one commandeered from the Kazaks. Bardolph had loaned his sword to the man he had sent back for us so that he would have the power to commandeer things.

And so we set off without Iskander, turning in our saddles to wave farewell to Velvet Trousers as he stood in the door of the yurt, his voluminous trousers flapping in the breeze and his new ring flashing on his finger. We picked up our caravan at their camping ground and traveled on to a tiny Chinese fort at the foot of the Muzart Pass.

The fort, called Hsia T'an Ying P'an, proved to be a small group of log buildings where a colonel and a detachment of men were stationed to guard the mouth of the pass and look after the Kirghiz and Kazaks of the neighborhood. All along the way people had spoken of Ma Ta Jen (literally "Big Man Ma"), the colonel, with a good deal of respect, and when we saw him we didn't wonder at it. He was a bluff and hearty old Chinese who spat with joy when he found that Owen could talk the talk of Tientsin, which he still called home though he had left there in a great hurry after the Boxer uprising of 1900 and hadn't been back since. He asked us to lunch on the spot and he and Owen talked steadily for four hours while it was being prepared. When the lunch arrived we wanted to spit for joy, too, for it contained fresh cabbage and green onions grown in a struggling little garden attached to the barracks, and after three weeks of a meat and rice diet they tasted like ambrosia.

After lunch he walked down with us to the grassy river bank where our tent had been pitched. He examined our belongings with a critical eye. A number of foreign travelers had stopped at his fort and he had a sophisticated knowledge of travel equipment. The Roosevelts had had a nicer tent and Mr. Morden had better field glasses, but none of them had had typewriters. He wanted us to take his photograph. The last visitors had photographed him and promised to send him copies but they had never arrived. Would we please write them a letter on our typewriter and ask them for the pictures?

He showed us letters he had received from Mr. Morden and from an English officer who had been hunting in the T'ien Shan and asked Owen to translate them for him. The "American Dukes," as everyone here calls the Roosevelts, had arrived with a great retinue and no Chinese interpreter and stayed three days. He had sent to Kulja for various expensive dainties on which to feast them but they (evidently wary of the mysteries of Chinese cooking) would only eat stewed mutton, the same kind of old stewed mutton that they could get at any old Kirghiz yurt.

Turkestan Reunion

He had a boil on his back when some foreign visitor was there, who had given him some medicine for it. He showed us the medicine, a little jar of bright pink hair pomade which he proceeded to rub assiduously into a pimple on his face.

Owen asked the Big Man if he had brought his family with him to live at the fort. "Well, I have one family here," he answered. "I suppose that you, too, have left the mother of your children in a more civilized place."

He assumed what all the other Chinese officials we have met have assumed, that I am merely a "traveling" wife and that of course Owen has a more respectable one at home. The Chinese would never expect a respectable married woman to take so rough a journey, and almost any Chinese who has to travel or live temporarily in the interior takes along a temporary traveling wife if he can afford it. They all think it very swell of Owen to have a traveling wife. "What a fine fellow," they say, "traveling with a Tientsin servant and a woman brought all the way from the coast!" But the Chinese officials who are settled in cities where they can have their regular families have never introduced me to their respectable wives. They have entertained me cordially with the men but the women never appear.

Here, however, where old Ma Ta Jen had a traveling wife, too, we were taken right into the bosom of the family. His wife was a pallid creature and had a much painted and beribboned little daughter. They lived in a two-room wooden house, the inner room where we had supper with them that night being ornately decorated with gaudy Khotan carpets and an elaborately draped *k'ang* and smelling strongly of cheap Chinese cosmetics.

At the fort Sheepo and Bardolph left us and we were not sorry to part with them. They had been so unsatisfactory that they deserved not to be tipped. However, it appeared at first as if Sheepo and the Ta Jen were bosom friends, and not wanting to appear ungrateful for his hospitality and also because we wanted him to give us a good guide for the rest of the journey, we tipped them both quite generously. Afterwards, however, Moses heard the soldiers saying that the Ta Jen knew that Sheepo was a rascal and that he had been worse than useless to us and made a lot of money out of it. The soldiers told him, too, what we had strongly suspected, that Sheepo had deliberately kept us from the Karagaitash so that he could smoke his opium and eat his mutton in comfortable yurts. He had made the Kazaks kill sheep for us so that he could have the skins, and had even insisted that they kill black sheep as black sheepskins are more valuable than white. He and Bardolph also made a lot of money out of commandeering horses. Everywhere they went they would threaten to commandeer, and the richer Kazaks would bribe them not to take their horses, so that for every horse they commandeered they got a lot of bribes for the ones they didn't.

The Big Man loved being lordly with his men, and every time he gave an order to an orderly he would curse and spit loudly after him as he went out of the room. We took some pictures of him in his grandest uniform, with sword and all the trimmings, mounted on a charging steed and with all his men lined up in the background.

Like most Chinese officials, he had done well out of taxes. He owned three thousand sheep, three hundred cows and one hundred horses, and he sent us off the next morning with lavish gifts of grain and rice, a sheep, and a splendid little riding pony to replace Iskander. The Gift Horse is a lively Kirghiz pony, strong but vicious. He seems like a little bug compared to the beautiful Iskander, but we're grateful for him just the same.

Riding through splattered sunshine up a winding wooded gorge we came to the yurts of the owner of our pack ponies at the edge of spruce forests and not far below the snows. Glittering snow peaks towered right above us, and we dallied, gorging on fresh milk and cream as thick as butter, while the pony men mended packs and harness, shod our new pony and laid in supplies for the Muzart.

Moses made us a big batch of scones for the journey and cooked the sheep that Big Man Ma had given us, assisted by a pretty girl whom we took to be the pony owner's daughter. Fido presented his boss's wife with an empty tomato can and was in high favor. Sadie, however, kept hanging around the door of our tent acting sullen, and we wondered why he didn't stay in the nice warm yurt with all the family, until we learned that the pretty girl in the yurt was not the boss's daughter at all, but Sadie's wife.

He had acquired her on the South Road on his last trip but she had absolutely refused to have anything to do with him and by the time he had got her back this far he had given up in despair and left her to serve the old lady. She seemed to do most of the work around the yurt, but she still refused to own the half wit Sadie for a husband, so he wouldn't go near her but stayed outside and sulked, boasting that when he got to the South Road this time he would buy another wife and bring her back here. Then this one would be sorry.

He was still muttering about it when we started up toward the snows on the last lap of our Heavenly Mountain journeyings. I'll always remember the grandeur of that day. We were soon above the trees and climbing over the feet of a dozen gorgeous glaciers up and up to the top of the watershed. The air was cool and golden and sparkling like champagne, and shimmering water from the melting snows rained down from the sheer rocky cliffs along the narrow trail.

Turkestan Reunion

About two in the afternoon we crossed over a ridge to a breathless view of towering ice peaks and glittering glaciers. For several miles the trail had led up through great boulders of white marble, and now across from us loomed an immense mountain of gleaming marble and glittering ice. Stretching to either side were other tall jagged ice peaks, and between us and them the ledge at our feet dropped sheer to a wide sea of tumbled glacier.

On the ledge were little patches of short bright green grass among the boulders, the last we were to see for several days, and remnants of camp fires and a great stench of the rotting corpses of ponies and donkeys which lay all about, half eaten by the vultures. Although it was still early the men said we must stop there for the night, as we would need the whole of the next day to cross the giant glacier, and that we must start before it was light the next morning in order to get over as much as possible of the snow and ice before the sun should begin to soften it and loosen avalanches.

The men had brought only a few sticks of firewood, so we had a scanty supper and started fireless and breakfastless the next morning in a cold and rainy dawn.

We had looked forward to the crossing of the Muzart as one of the most difficult of all the feats of our travels. I have really been almost disappointed that we haven't had more hardships on this trip. I don't mean just cold and heat, which one can have almost anywhere, but interesting and adventurous hardships which give one a sense of being able to endure and conquer. Crossing the Muzart, however, did not prove disappointingly easy, even after all the wild tales we had heard about its difficulties and dangers.

It rained all day, a cold wet penetrating rain which cast a blue gloom over the giant glacier. We had to slide down snow slides on our bowhinds and jump fissures in the green ice on horseback and the Gift Horse gave me a vicious kick when I was trying to egg him into sliding down an icy cliff on *his* bowhind. I had never dreamed of such a place.

We climbed for hours over heaps of ice and boulders as high as a house, as high as a skyscraper, the path marked by carcasses and decaying bodies of dead horses and donkeys. We skirted fissures and holes in the ice as large and deep as houses, sheer walls of green ice with rushing water at the bottom. At last we came to the far edge of the mammoth glacier, to a high rocky cliff where Owen saw an ibex on the skyline and shot it, the report of his rifle echoing and reechoing and starting roaring avalanches in the dark mountains.

We had crossed the width of the glacier but it was still necessary to descend several miles to its snout. At its far edge we came to a tiny hut on the side of the cliff where two Chantos stayed to watch the trail, to cut steps in the ice and to help horses down the steepest of the ice slides. We crawled into their hut to get a little dry and warm. Then for hours we scrambled over what looked like a nightmare of all the municipal ash dumps of all the giants in the world, gray gravel, rocks, boulders heaped house high, skyscraper high. Just below the surface of the loose gray gravel was slippery ice. The ponies slid along as best they could. I frequently resorted to hands and knees. It was good sport but I was rather wrecked when we reached the bottom.

Even then we couldn't stop, for at the bottom was a wide flat gravel river bed between beetling cliffs, very different from the smiling flowery meadows and cool forests on the other side. There was neither grass nor firewood, and the ponies had had nothing to eat the night before. The pony men said that if we kept on till dark we would come to some grass and fuel. If it hadn't been for that I couldn't have gone a step farther. Just at the bottom of the glacier, however, our nice guide found a cave where someone had left a few sticks of firewood. He built a fire and we managed to get a little dry and warm before plodding on.

Our guide had proved himself to be as nice as possible. He was a Kirghiz who spoke good Chinese and had been with the Roosevelts and with Morden and Clark. He knew the road and how to care for horses, was much the handiest man we have had about camp and was quite a delightful person all together.

Turkestan Reunion

After we left the cave we went on endlessly, looking for the grass. The way was weird and beautiful. First we had to ford the river and it was deep and swift and difficult. Then we went on and on between high swirls of cliffs of all deep shades of red and purple, and once we saw a flock of ibex leaping along on what looked like a perfectly perpendicular surface.

In a desolate stretch that looked as if no man had ever seen it we were startled to come suddenly upon an old Chanto. He was standing forlornly by the road waiting for us to come up to him. He held out a wooden Mongol bowl and started begging in a sing song chant. The guide questioned him and he managed to explain that he was trying to get home to Kashgar, having lost all his money in Kulja, but that the water ahead was too big for him to cross and he had eaten all his bread. We told him to come along with us.

Then, more and more surprising, pretty soon we met another man, this time a young Chinese half out of his head with cold and fright. He was on his way to Kulja, and in crossing the swift river his coat and shoes and all his food had been swept away in the current and he had nearly drowned. If we hadn't come along he might well have frozen or starved before he could get to any help, so we took him along with us, too.

At last we came to the little patch of grass. But alas it was on the other side of the river and the water here was too deep and swift to ford. We wanted to weep for the ponies, but we couldn't go any farther. The Good Guide set the two beggars to work gathering what little desert scrub there was for firewood, but it was all wet from the drizzling rain and we couldn't get it lit. "Take the beggar's wooden bowl," suggested the Chinese youth. "He's a Chanto. What right has he to a Mongol bowl?" And before we could stop him the guide was shaving it onto the fire, his one idea being to get us warm. It did start the fire and soon we had a good blaze and were warm if not dry by the time the packs arrived.

When the poor old Chanto discovered that his bowl was gone he heaped ashes on his head and called on Allah to witness his abuse. We soon realized that he was a madman, a perfectly harmless madman. We gave him an empty tomato tin to replace his bowl and he was quite happy. He followed us for two days and the men seemed to like to have him, as madmen are considered holy. They helped him over all the swift rivers we crossed the next day, Fido always leading a pony back for him to ride. They also made good use of him. As soon as we got to camp it was, "Madman, gather wood," or "Madman, fetch some water," but after all the work was done, until late in the night, they would sit around the camp fire and listen to him preach. He knew miles of the Koran by heart which he would recite to them and chant

246

weird prayers. He also told their fortunes and they seemed to take him very seriously.

The Chinese chap was going in the other direction and all the men helped to fit him out for his journey, very generously giving him food and clothing, though to be sure it was mostly out of our stores. The Good Guide, however, gave him his only high boots. "Why did you do that?" asked Owen, for the guide had told him that he knew the man and that he was not at all a good man. To which the Good Guide replied, "Alas, his wickedness does not enable him to walk across the Muzart without good boots, and I can buy another pair in Aksu."

We had another long day of rocky paths and raging fords before we came to any grass and even then it was very scant, as the good grass was all across the big river. We had brought oats for our riding ponies but no hay, and being unaccustomed to eating oats they got woefully thin. And the pack ponies had nothing at all but a few scraggly weeds for two whole days.

Beyond the first grass we came to the mouth of the valley and a small Chinese barracks, and beyond that a Chanto village where we took shelter from a rainstorm. Camp that night was in a meadow with poor grass and no fuel, but the next day, after a long early morning march through hot red salt hills of strange formation we came to a tiny oasis and took refuge in a cool green apricot orchard where we ate green apricots while our ponies ate large bundles of real hay.

Leaving that cool oasis the Gift Horse went quite lame. We had started on a long desert march where we couldn't stop to rest him, and to make matters worse we got caught in a nasty sandstorm. But by dark we came to a town. There the Good Guide offered to cure the Bug by sending his lameness into the earth. He held a knotted rope on the thigh of the lame leg, and with a hammer hit the knot lightly, then hit the earth, hit the knot and then the earth a number of times. "Tomorrow it will still be lame," he said, "and the day after that it will be all right." Owen was skeptical. He thought the pony was permanently lamed and that we might as well leave him in Aksu. But the guide was right. He seems to have quite recovered.

From the town, which had the delightful name of Jam, they told us it was forty li to Aksu, but the forty turned out to be a long hot ninety across sand desert. Just outside the city we came across a strange little creature which Owen recognized, or thought he did, from his dictionary reading, as a "djerboa or kangaroo rat." He had very large ears and very long hind legs and went hopping about in a most comical way. He was just a baby and Owen christened him Lawrence and put him in his saddle bag. Later he took him to call on the governor here, who was charmed with him. He played with him for hours in his garden and then borrowed him for a day so that he could show him to his wife. The servants found a little basket for him to live in and have tried hard to find out what he liked to eat, but poor little Lawrence wasted away and died. Owen wanted to pickle him and take him home in a bottle, but Moses wouldn't let him. We had letters from Pan to friends of his here and are staying with the postmaster. We have reason again to bless the "great god Pan." His name seems to work miracles all over the province, and his two special friends in Aksu, a merchant and the postmaster, seem honored to wait on us hand and foot because we are friends of his. They have long conferences as to what we should be given to eat, and every few minutes come in with plates of apricots or melons. They evidently made great preparations for our coming, putting new covers on the *k'ang* and quilts and making new *k'ang* curtains.

The merchant and the postmaster are both "Tientsin men," so Moses is having a great time with them. Being a Tientsin man Moses is treated as an equal by most of the Chinese we meet. Even Ma Ta Jen invited him to supper.

The Good Guide has just been in to say good-by. Owen gave him a splendid letter of recommendation, ten taels and a pair of field glasses. Whereupon he pulled the heavy silver ring from his middle finger and presented it to me, saying that it was the only thing he had to give and he hoped I would accept it. I was thrilled as Owen had been casting envious eyes at it for days. Of course, like Velvet Trousers' dutiful wife, I turned it over to my lord as soon as the giver's back was turned. It has an octagonal seal with the guide's name in Arabic characters and is really stunning-looking.

Soon after we arrived Owen went to call on the officials, and he hadn't been gone a minute before the postmaster's wife, mother and two babies came in to see me. I showed them all our belongings and they stayed all the time he was gone, but the minute they heard him come in the gate they were off like rabbits. And it has been the same way ever since. They won't come in the room as long as Owen is here, but pop in the minute he leaves.

There is a delightful old governor here who invited us to a feast this morning in his gardens. The gardens were spacious and beautiful and filled with every kind of flower imaginable, many of them imported from other countries. He has a big summer house by a lotus pond in which he spends much of his time. He has known all the explorers and foreign travelers who have visited Turkestan, and talked delightfully. The other guests were the *hsien* magistrate, who had called on us before breakfast, and our host the postmaster.

The *hsien* magistrate has secured us a cart for our trip to Kashgar for twenty-two silver taels. It is an eighteen-stage journey and the cheapest one we have had yet.

CHAPTER XIV. *Of the long South Road through deserts and oases and of how we traveled it from Aksu to Kashgar, of more moonlit deserts and mud inns, a witch dance, a runaway wife, and a pretty traveling companion.*

Kashgar

July 21

DEAR FAMILY,

AFTER fifteen breathless sticky vaga-
bond days of desert we have reached an oasis of civilization, of all Central Asia the most civilized, British India
transplanted to Turkestan, the British Consulate General in Kashgar. For the first time in our travels we
have arrived ahead of schedule, not because we traveled
fast but because we were misinformed as to the length of
the journey, and our host and hostess are still in the hills.
They will be back in a few days, however, and they left
cordial word for us to make ourselves at home in their
guest house. We are loving the contrast of its comfort
with our recent vagabondage—hot baths, clean sheets,
dainty food, nice dishes, white-robed servants, a library
of books, shady terraces and an enchanting garden riotous
with fruit and flowers.

Nothing could be better calculated to make us appreciate the joys and beauties of the British Consulate General than the journey from Aksu to Kashgar. In Aksu we
had found a letter from the consul, forwarded to us from

Turkestan Reunion

Urumchi, in which he urged us to come to Kashgar sooner or later but not in July or early August, as the road from Aksu was a purgatory of heat and mosquitos. But even if we had had his letter in Urumchi we couldn't have altered our plans, and the only thing to do was to arrange to make the journey with as little discomfort as possible.

The heat was so unbearable that we traveled entirely at night, in the most neat, sweet and delightful cart you can imagine. It was a "house-cart," a sort of Wendy house on wheels, and it had been built for Postmaster Wang in which to bring his pretty wife from Urumchi to Aksu. At least he had had the top built to fit onto any ordinary Turkestan wagon.

We covered the bottom of the cart with our boxes and bags, then spread on them everything soft we had, tent, furs, felts and sleeping bags, with a clean cover over them all and cushions at the back. On top of this was placed the floorless little hut. It was perhaps six feet wide by seven feet long by four feet high, all lined with felt, with a screened window at the back which had a little curtain that rolled up and down, and screened double doors at the front, also with a curtain and a little latch, a sort of dog kennel de luxe.

Wang T'ai-t'ai had washed the blue curtains for us and the blue canopy at the front that served as an awning, and all the neighbors came to watch us load up on the road in front of the house. Postmaster Wang sent us off laden with gifts, two tiny jade bowls, a sack of dried apricots, a bag of fine salt crystals from the hills near Aksu, and more melons than we could carry.

We were appalled at the money we had to take with us. In Aksu we changed our Kulja money to Kashgar money. The Kashgar currency is the only silver currency in the province, a tael being worth three Urumchi taels, or about sixty cents gold. There was very little silver to be had in Aksu, and no paper, so that we had to carry most of our fortune in copper, an immense sack full, some of it in cash, four hundred to the tael. Moses had a munificent time along the road dispensing coppers by the yard.

We set out in splendid cavalcade. Our driver was a gentle toothless old man who owned two carts, our big cart and a smaller one. As we had hired only one of his carts, and he was afraid to leave the other in Aksu, it was to come with us, driven by a boy of about fifteen, and Moses was scheming to bribe a ride in it where he could snooze more comfortably than he could perched on the front of ours.

In spite of the heat we had to leave Aksu in mid-afternoon, as the Qum Ariq River, eight or ten miles away, was in flood and must be crossed before dark. Besides our two carts we had two soldiers who led our riding ponies. One was a rabbity pockmarked youth and the other looked like an opium-sodden wreck. The governor also sent extra escorts and a very nice Turki official to see us safely across the river, and Postmaster Wang came with us in a Peking cart as far as the ford.

We reached the wide river at dusk and there was a great bustle of loading us all on and off the flat-bottomed ferry and saying good-by to the official and our hosts. At the river Moses was disconcerted to discover that the little cart he had plotted to ride in contained a passenger, a pretty girl of about sixteen with a naked brown baby. The old carter explained that he had picked her up at the last minute and that her husband was sending her home to her mother because of her bad temper. The old man was afraid to leave his boy driver to her charms and so drove her himself and gave the boy to us. This kept causing delays and disasters, as the youngster was much too lively to sleep in the daytime and so couldn't keep awake at night when he was driving, and was always getting us stuck in ditches and almost capsizing us.

On such occasions the usually mild old man would work and tug for a bit at the cart and then turn on the kid with a stream of swearing and spit scornfully in his face. Turki swearing is marvelous, all through the nose and teeth in a sort of June Bug effect.

It was dark when we set out from the river, and all the first stage was over irrigated land, which made us abandon vain hopes that we might be able to sleep in the cart. The smaller irrigation ditches were great ruts across the road that jolted us with a bang to the roof or hard against the wall. The larger ditches were bridged, with no attempt to slope the road up to the bridge, so that there was a high step at either end. With much cracking of whips and shouting of "Oa, oa, oa," the drivers would urge the horses up onto the bridge with a tremendous jolt. Then we would hold our breaths till we had bumped off the other end and before we could get to sleep we would be at another bridge. We did find later, though, that on the soft sandy roads through the desert we could sleep very well.

To add to our discouragement that first night there was a duststorm which covered us and everything in the cart and filled our eyes and mouths and noses with an uncomfortable grit. At about two in the morning we pulled into the dark yard of an inn. The soldiers built a little fire and made us some tea and Moses made an attempt at brushing the dust out of the cart and brought us buckets of water to wash in and we undressed and went to bed in our little house, the floor of which was fairly flat and soft.

About six Moses wakened us and suggested that we move into the inn before our cart became an oven. He and the soldiers had swept out a cool dark little room, sprinkled it all with water and lined it with felts. We took in cushions, books, papers and typewriter and prepared to spend the day. Moses brought us a breakfast of melons, apricots, scrambled eggs, crisp Chanto bread and tea. All day we had plenty of fruit and cold water and managed to keep fairly comfortable, though the day outside was sizzling.

We lived this way for fifteen days. We bought an immense new white felt which would completely cover the *k'ang* of any inn room. As soon as it was light Moses and the soldiers would clean and sprinkle a room for us. Then, before it was hot we would waken in the cart and hand out to Moses the things we wanted during the day and in a few minutes we would hop down and into our room and find it ready for us, felts, cushions, books, a big bowl of fruit and buckets and bowls of water for baths. After baths we'd put on fresh pajamas and bellow for breakfast and then loaf all day, eating another meal about four. Often the thermometer climbed to the 100 mark in our room, but we comforted ourselves that it was very much hotter outside.

Sometimes we would dress about five, Owen in shorts and cotton shirt and I in cotton riding clothes. Then the cart would go off without us and we would wait till the cool began, perhaps at seven, and ride for two or three hours until we caught the cart, clamber in, change into pajamas, spread clean sheets on the soft floor of the cart and sleep as well as possible till morning found us again in an inn yard.

Turkestan Reunion

A few times we rode all night on the ponies across dim deserts, or clambered out in the night if we couldn't sleep and rode in our pajamas. Oftener at midnight we would come to the halfway stage, a sleeping hamlet or just an inn by the roadside, and we would waken the innkeeper and ask for tea and then sleep in our clothes till the cart caught up to us. I always loved these inn yards in the night with the dim shapes of carts and horses and the black stables where one could hear more horses stirring, the red coals of supper fires in corners of the courtyard and sometimes white-clad figures asleep on outdoor *k'angs*.

Once, at midnight in a tiny village, we found a fruit seller sitting cross-legged under a huge umbrella behind a mammoth pile of apricots, sorting them by the light of a tiny torch, the flickering glow from which turned his brown face exactly the color of his apricots. We bought a bandana full and ate them while we were waiting for the cart.

There was fruit at almost every stage, melons and apricots and, toward the end, delicious juicy nectarines. During one hot day Moses kept count of our apricot pits and reported that we'd each eaten a hundred. There were no evil effects.

During the first stages of our journey we blessed Postmaster Wang a hundred times, for he had sent word to mail carriers along the way to look after us and they not only brought us melons on stages where melons don't grow but on several occasions carried water many miles for us on stages where the water was undrinkable. They carried it in immense gourds by strings around the narrow necks. Gourds are used for everything. Men riding across the desert carry gourds of water tied to their donkeys or ponies, they make bowls of them and water-pipes and use tiny ones for snuff and tobacco.

There are several stages of the road where the water is scant and too bitter to drink and we thought about how it wasn't many miles away, out on the Taklamakan desert which we were skirting, that Sven Hedin's companions died of thirst.

I should love to travel that road in the spring or fall when it isn't so hot. The first hundred miles from Aksu are along or very close to the old Silk Road built by a Han emperor in the second century B.C. on which silk was carried by caravan to Persia and sold beyond Persia to the Greeks and the Romans.

They tell us that in the autumn in the Tarim jungle there are many kinds of small game, but now almost nothing lives and nothing grows. Melons will grow in soil too salty for anything else, but aside from melon patches and orchards in the oases there is little cultivation. We saw signs of vain attempts at extensive irrigation between Aksu and Maralbashi. A ditch had been dug along the road for many miles and our rabbity soldier told us that it had taken several years and several fortunes to prepare and that when it was all ready at last the water was turned into it and promptly sunk into the sand. It wouldn't hold a drop.

Our rabbity soldier, by the way, turned out to be most awfully nice. He had a white pony of which he was very proud. He had bought it as a tiny colt and brought it up himself and he spent hours every day grooming it. He always groomed our ponies, too, quite on his own initiative, and seemed to enjoy it. Our little Bug continues to try to give us vicious kicks whenever we go near him, but Rabbity Soldier says that if he grooms him every day he will become quite tame.

I have three particularly vivid memories of this journey from Aksu to Kashgar: one of a witch dance, one of a runaway wife being caught by her husband, and one of a wash day at an inn when our pretty traveling companion exhibited her temper.

About noon of our first day out of Aksu we heard a tremendous din of cymbals and drums and shouting across the courtyard of the inn and Moses came in to tell us that the villagers were having a devil dance. If the temperature of that courtyard had been below 100 in the shade, and if there had been any shade in the courtyard, this would have excited us greatly. As it was we agreed that a devil dance by the Dalai Lama himself could not tempt us out of our dark little hole. So we stayed put for an hour or two, trying to read and write to the accompaniment of drums and cymbals and loud chanting. It wasn't that we were being blasé about devil dances, but only too drugged with the heat. However, it was a most insistent chant with a weird regular rhythm that held our attention in spite of ourselves. Every once in awhile it seemed to work up into a perfect frenzy accompanied by wild shouting, so that we became "curiouser and curiouser" and finally ventured out to see what was happening.

Villagers and carters were crowding around the door and windows of the largest room in the inn, and they good-naturedly made room for us to peek through a window at one of the strangest sights I have ever seen. In the center of the room a rope stretched from the smoke hole in the ceiling to the floor, and at the foot of the rope knelt a woman clothed in many layers of white cotton and with heavy white muslin veils over her head. She was holding the rope with both hands and swaying gently to the rhythm of the chant. All about the woman the room was full of white-clad men beating drums and clanging cymbals and chanting as if their lives depended on it. But the outstanding figure in the room was a large handsome woman who seemed to be conducting a ceremony, evidently a sort of witch doctor.

At first she had cymbals which she clashed wildly close to the head and body of the woman clinging to the rope, accompanied all the while by frenzied chanting. Then she took a dagger and as the chant grew wilder she plunged it into the air all about the woman until after a final great clash of the cymbals she stabbed her in the heart. The woman was so thickly padded with clothing that the dagger did not actually pierce her, and when it was withdrawn she pulled herself up by the rope and started swinging slowly round it. As the music accelerated she went faster and faster until finally she was whirling around it like a mad dervish. Eventually she became so dizzy that she let go of the rope and went hurling across the room, sinking in a heap against the opposite wall.

At this the witch doctor rushed toward her brandishing the dagger and stabbed it into the wall all around her, leaving it finally stuck into the mud and wattle just above her head. Then she seized a whip and cracked it in the air all about the woman, after which she rushed about the room slashing at everyone and everything and out the door into the courtyard, scattering the crowd. I had to jump quickly to escape being hit, much to the amusement of the villagers.

So far as we could make out from the spectators we could ask, the swathed and veiled woman was ill and the witch doctor was attempting to chase the devils from her, frightening and stabbing them and lashing them out of the room. The rope was to act as a conductor by which the devils could escape through the smoke hole.

Turkestan Reunion

Some days later at a little inn we heard a great chatter and clatter in the room next to ours, and this time we didn't need to brave the sun to see what was happening as there was a hole in the mud wall between the two rooms. I peeked through it to see a whole sewing circle of village women all talking at once. On a stool in the center of the group was a young girl, her face pretty but tear-stained. One woman was busily combing the girl's hair and braiding it into long smooth black plaits and others were fussing about with clothes. At the same time across the courtyard we could hear men's voices talking excitedly.

We appealed to Moses, who has large ears for gossip, and he told us that the young girl had run away from her husband with another man and had arrived at our inn early that morning. Not long afterwards the irate husband appeared upon the scene and insisted on dragging his erring wife home with him. In true Oriental fashion, where in the absence of law courts the public is always the judge, the villagers had all gathered to decide the fate of the girl and her lover. They all agreed that she should return to her husband if he were so foolish as to want her back again, and the women were busy getting her ready and all vying with each other to cheer her up and point the moral.

Between the two men matters were evidently not settled. They had appealed to Moses, as the only available member of the ruling race, to act as judge, but he had characteristically declined to become involved.

Women are so plentiful among the Turkis that the villagers were doubtless telling the girl that she should feel flattered that her husband wanted her back. For a Turki nothing is easier to acquire or to dispense with than a wife. A woman is usually expected to provide a complete trousseau, household utensils and often a money dowry, but all the husband has to do is to go before a *mullah* and pay him a tael or two to perform the simplest of marriage ceremonies. And when he gets tired of his wife he sends her home. He can obtain a divorce simply by going to a magistrate, without his wife's presence or consent, and paying two taels. Some men get new wives every few months. A man may not only change wives as often as he likes but may have as many as four at one time. We heard yesterday of a middle-aged Mohammedan British subject who had had over sixty and was still going strong.

The girl, however, who usually marries first at the age of twelve or thirteen, cannot obtain a divorce without her husband's consent. All she can do is to run away and hope that he will divorce her. If he does she can marry again after one hundred days. Sometimes she pays her husband a large sum to divorce her, and it may have been the omission of this part of the ceremony that made our neighbor's husband so irate. The court was still in full session when we left that afternoon, so we never heard what happened to the lover.

An entertaining account of Turkestan marriage occurs in *Servant of Sahibs,* the autobiography of a Ladakhi who traveled with a number of foreigners in Southern Turkestan. I will copy it out for you, as it shows very vividly the attitude of organized religion.

"And everybody was singing in our camp.

"In Chinese Turkestan it has been the custom that any man can marriage for ten days, a month, or for one day, for as many days as he wanted. But unless a *mullah* does read *nika,* one will not find any wives. Now all our men made marriage there. Some my friends married three or four times. Now I wanted to marry one. And to our camp came an old woman who washed sahib's clothes and ours. That woman knew Abdurahman. When Abdurahman had come to Khotan with French sahibs, at that time that woman had washed their clothes, and she had helped for the marriage for all servants of sahibs. Besides the servants the elder French sahib had marriage also for a long time. That all arrangement had made this old woman also. Now she arranged for us our marriage. I told that woman: 'I want to marry with a girl who has not any sickness.'

"After sahibs' dinner, Kalam Rassul and I went to that old woman's house. There had gathered many girls. All were sitting by wall in that room. Now that old woman said to us: 'Among them, which is your choice, tell me.' But there were no one so beautiful as Ladaki girls. But they were not bad. Now Kalam Rassul pointed out one girl. He said: 'That one I like.' I showed one; then all the other girls went to their homes. The two girls, which we chose, were brought before the *mullah*. There brought some breads, and, in a cup, salty water. These were kept in front of the *mullah* on a *dastarkhan*. Then the *mullah* read some words of Koran, then took a piece of bread, put it in that salty water, and gave to me and to that girl, and for Kalan Rassul made the same. Then we gave one *tanga*, each man, to the *mullah*. Before the *mullah* reading with girl, promise that twenty *tanga* to given the girl. (But the Khotan *tanga* is two *tanga* of Yarkand.)

"Three days after, I let go my cheap wife. I did not like to keep longer, and I gave her *tangas* twenty as that which we had promised. Besides that I gave her a good hat, and some clothes. She was glad to get in three days all that things. From that day I do not like to have that kind of wife."

The nomad women in the mountains have a much better time than the women in the oasis villages, as there aren't enough of them to go around and they are much sought after. A man may have to pay fifty head of cattle for a wife, and she can divorce him at any time by returning the purchase price, which rather gives her the upper hand; but she leads a hard life, milking the sheep, goats, cows, and mares as well as preparing the food and tending to the taking down and pitching of their white felt tents on all the migrations, so that she deserves all the freedom and authority that she can get. In some regions it is customary for a Kazak boy first to marry a woman older than himself, to guide his footsteps in married life. Then, some ten years later, he weds a younger wife, and his earlier spouse is relegated to the position of dowager.

A few days before we reached Kashgar I was loafing on an out of door *k'ang* in an inn yard, watching some Turki women washing clothes in large shallow wooden tubs. A husky woman brought water in gourds from a ditch outside the inn while several others scrubbed and rinsed and poured the dirty water into a hole they had dug in the ground. From the color of the water it must have been an annual occasion, and they were making a day of it.

The country people usually wear but two garments in the summer, loose trousers and a sort of long loose coat, the men's garments being white and belted in with a long wide cotton sash which they twist and wind about their waists, while the women's are often of red or gay flowered print and flow nightgown fashion from the shoulders. The women wear their hair in long shiny black plaits and when they go out throw a large white veil over their heads. Some of these veils were being washed and looked as big as sheets when they were hung out to dry. In the cities the men often wear striped cotton coats when the weather gets cooler and the women sleeveless jackets, but in the villages they add padded cotton coats, with sheepskins for the great cold.

Suddenly there were shrill voices followed by sobs, tears and loud wailing on the other side of the courtyard and all the women dropped their laundry and rushed to see what was happening. There was a village crowd gathered around our pretty fellow passenger, who wasn't at the moment looking in the least pretty but was sitting in the dust hugging her knees and sobbing and wailing and hurling invectives at a handsome carter who had just driven into the yard.

I knew that Moses would soon appear with an explanation, and sure enough he did. It seems that the girl had just been divorced by her husband and was on her way home to her mother. She had come from her husband's home in Kucha as far as Aksu with the handsome carter, who had refused to take her any farther because he said she had too bad a temper. So she had paid him nothing and hired our old man to take her the rest of the way. And now the handsome carter, having caught up with her, was telling the village things about her private life she didn't like to hear. Whether her emotions were somewhat involved with the handsome carter or whether it was just that she didn't like to lose face so near home, she was evidently much upset and fairly let herself go for the rest of the afternoon, sobbing and crying and rolling about in the dust, and no one could comfort her.

Turkestan Reunion

Her two-year-old baby played about the yard quite unconcernedly. He was an adorable child and very friendly, coming into our room whenever he could and always running to take hold of my hand or jump into my arms whenever he saw me in the yard.

We reached Maralbashi, the largest town on the road, on a weekly market day, and everything was carnival. Our hot inn was crowded with a troupe of Chinese actors. The *hsien* magistrate, hearing of our arrival, sent us gifts of tinned biscuits, eggs, and cigarettes. And knowing what excitement would be created by the appearance of two foreigners in the crowded market-place he also sent two *yamen* runners to escort us on a pilgrimage through the market.

I think markets are fun in any land, but for color and picturesqueness and gaiety no markets can rival those of Turkestan. The streets were as jammed as the Times Square subway station at the rush hour, and the *yamen* runners had to push ahead of us and beat off the crowds with large sticks so that we could move at all. The stalls were sheltered with umbrella awnings, beneath which were heaps of melons or apricots or rounds of bread, gay saddle bags or studded harness or rows of copper pots, festoons of colored cotton cloth or bundles of lucerne for ponies. There were vendors of cold drinks of a vicious pink color, and fortune tellers, musicians and story-tellers, but we were the biggest show of all.

Faizabad, two stages nearer Kashgar, we also reached on market day, but it was a tiny town with a peaceful market along the two sides of its shady canopied street.

Two days later, as soon as it was light, we saw that we were approaching the Chinese city of Kashgar, which is the seat of the Chinese administration and is five miles from the Turki city of Kashgar where we are living. We dressed and deserted the cart for our ponies in time to see its gates and towers as we skirted the outer wall.

New escorts joined us at the Chinese city and we rode in cavalcade along the shady avenue which leads through irrigated fields and villages from the Chinese to the Turki city. We rode through the city gate and wound through streets still sleeping, all the way across the picturesque old town and out a far gate and past some Russian buildings and up to a gate adorned with lion and unicorn. Inside we found warm welcome from the Chinese and Indian secretaries of the consulate, the guest house ready for us, stacks of mail and a good English breakfast.

CHAPTER XV. *Of the storied city of Kashgar and the comforts of the British Consulate General, of how we became Sahib and Mem Sahib and are too polite to an Aksakal. Of how we set out with Tashi and his ponies to cross the Five High Passes on the highest and most difficult trade route in the world.*

Leh, Ladakh

September 15

DEAR FAMILY,

T HIS letter is to be about the most difficult and exciting and adventurous of all of our travels,
probably the most exciting and adventurous journey we'll
ever make in our lives. I haven't written to you for nearly
two months and I do hope that you will understand that
it isn't because I haven't thought about you every day but
because it took every ounce of strength I had to get
through with each day's traveling.

Getting out of Chinese Turkestan has been even more
difficult than getting in, which adds considerably to our
feeling of having spent our extended honeymoon on another planet altogether. For Turkestan, like the princess
in the fairy tale, will always seem more alluring because
of the tangled forests and the dragon to be slain.

I wrote you last in Kashgar, on the other planet. We
spent two weeks there with the charming British Consul
General and his wife, reveling in the comforts of the
consulate, exploring Kashgar, and preparing for the journey to India. Kashgar is a mud town, like all the other

275

towns of Central Asia, but larger and gayer, with a more splendid bazaar and more pretentious mosques. The days there passed too quickly. Owen paid and received official calls. Moses picked fruit from the trees and made jam. I repacked, and refurbished our wardrobes, and, as Moses expressed it, we all walked about and stared. My one regret now is that Owen isn't an Englishman so that he might one day aspire to be a consul in Kashgar.

In Kashgar we were being comparatively civilized, but there was still between us and India this most adventurous part of our journey. The Karakorum route which we were setting out to follow is said to be the highest and most difficult trade route in the world. From Yarkand to Leh is a month's hard traveling over mountain passes five of which are over 16,000 feet. The British consul told us that caravans average a loss of forty per cent of their animals on this road, swept away by swift rivers, falling over cliffs, or weakened from altitude and insufficient food. And not only is it a test of endurance for men but often they cannot stand the altitude and become seriously ill.

"How do you know that you can stand the altitude?" everyone asked us in Peking before we started. And we didn't know. I had visions of myself slung unconscious over the back of a pony while we crossed the Karakoram, 18,300 feet above sea level. This was by no means the

first time on our journey from Peking to India that we
had to take a chance.

We sold our ponies in Kashgar, for we couldn't bear to
submit them to the rigors of that road. Meander was in
perfect condition and the Chinese secretary at the consulate was very pleased to buy him from us for exactly
what we had paid for him in Urumchi. Our luggage we
cut to the minimum and transferred to strong new pony
boxes, wood covered with yak hide and bound with iron;
and on the first of August we went forth, traveling the
five days from Kashgar to Yarkand by cart on a pleasant
road where the oases were leafier and not so far apart
as they had been farther north.

We had left behind all those enchanted places which
I was the first white woman to see. In Kashgar there
had been the consul's wife and several Swedish missionaries, and two days from Kashgar again we found a missionary couple in the town of Yangi Hissar. Englishmen
come over from India to shoot in the Pamirs. This year
one of them even brought his wife. We met them in a garden in Posgam. They had bathtubs and thirteen servants.
Our Moses said he was going to strike for thirteen sal-
aries. From Kashgar we became Sahib and Mem Sahib,
and were treated no longer as curiosities but as members
of the Ruling Race, which was fun but needed living
up to.

As Sahib and Mem Sahib our approach was grandly

heralded, and the village longbeards rode forth to meet us, spreading by the road a *dasturkhan,* which is a table-cloth all set out with tea, and small dishes of nuts and raisins, fruits and sticky-looking sweets. When we came to inns we found rugs spread for us and heaping bowls of fruit, and at Yarkand we were led to a most beauteous garden where we camped in a summer house in the midst of a riot of summer flowers and fruit.

The garden belonged to the British Aksakal, I think he was an Afghan, who was head of the British subjects, mostly Indian traders and money lenders, who had settled at Yarkand.

Aksakal means white beard (or, consequently, "elder") but he had a black beard and narrow eyes and we didn't get on with him very well. He was the first of the breed we had encountered and we made the mistake of treating him as we treated Chinese officials, with deference and respect. The Chinese appreciated this attitude, entertaining us with feasts and making us presents and, as our hosts, trying to see that we weren't cheated and arranging our transport as cheaply as possible. To the Aksakal, however, who was evidently completely unaccustomed to deference from the "ruling race," our courtesy seemed a weakness of which he could take advantage, and he pocketed exorbitant commissions for himself on everything we bought in Yarkand, our supplies for the journey to Leh and the hire of the fourteen ponies and four men who formed our caravan. Later, we heard from a British officer here that an Aksakal, far from having the dignity of a Chinese official, was a person to whom you gave orders, and whom you could tip, like a butler.

In Yarkand we also found missionaries, a Swedish couple who were most helpful in assisting us with our preparations.

Our caravan proved a great success, and the four Ladakhis the most delightful and efficient transport men we had encountered anywhere. They were big strapping merry fellows and the greater the hardships of the road the more they sang and joked. They wore pigtails and turquoise earrings and black and white rope shoes that turned up in a great swirl like gondolas at the toes. They were caked with dirt, of course, like all Tibetans. They could speak only about as much broken Turki as we could, so that our animated conversations always caused much merriment.

The ponies were pasturing several days away toward the mountains, so that we set out from Yarkand in covered wagons and with only two of the men, Tashi, the headman, who walked in the lead tootling cheerily on a wooden flute, and a great ourang-outang of a fellow, whom we dubbed Hairy Harry, bringing up the rear.

We had learned our lesson about Aksakals, and in the few towns left to visit we were rather snooty and they seemed to like it better. Outside Kargalik we were met on the road by all the leading citizens, and in front of the Aksakal's garden they had hung a great banner with WELCOME sewed on it in irregular letters, and a great *dasturkhan* was waiting for us.

For three long desert days from Kargalik to Sanju Bazaar we traveled with a string of camels, and at Sanju we found our ponies and the other two men, who came out to meet us with offerings of nosegays. We camped there in a shady garden for two days while the men worked busily patching tent, harness and pack saddles.

In the T'ien Shan we had had only seven ponies and two men, but here loads must be lighter because of the altitude, and we had to carry a month's rations for ourselves and men and grain for the ponies, as practically nothing could be bought on the way and there are a number of days on that road where there is no grazing at all. On some stages we even had to carry fuel for our camp fire, so that fourteen ponies proved not one too many.

It was rather a scraggly-looking outfit, scrawny unkempt-looking little ponies with wisps of mane hanging in bangs over their bright eyes and looking like big-winged little bats under our pairs of big black pony boxes. Their big loads seemed not to squelch them in the least, however, and, bred to the altitude, they were much hardier for that road than the larger and huskier-looking Turkestan ponies would have been.

Turkestan Reunion

We set out regretfully from Sanju Bazaar, the last little oasis in Chinese Turkestan, eager for the unknown adventures which lay waiting for us beyond the ranges but reluctant to leave behind us the magic land which had given us so perfect a honeymoon.

Two things more alluring than a mountain range to cross are three mountain ranges to cross, three big ones subdivided into range after range of the highest mountains in the world. I suppose one should really cross them from India toward Turkestan, where the lure of strange lands beyond is added to the stimulation of conquering each difficult pass as it comes. To be sure, we have never been to India but we know it is full of trains and motor cars and Englishmen and Thomas Cooks, and each range that we crossed put one more barrier between us and the Central Asia that we loved. But, on the other hand, after crossing the mountains, any other traveling in Turkestan would seem pretty tame, and it was rather gorgeous to have the Five High Passes as a thrilling climax.

The first of the five is the Sanju Dawan, 16,600 feet, (*dawan* is Turki for "pass"). After four days of climbing through tumbled red and copper canyons and over the Chuchu Dawan, which doesn't seem to count as a high pass though its crest is some 14,000 feet and made us all puff and pant aplenty, we rode one late afternoon up into wide fans of apple-green meadow just below the pale blue snows, a steep amphitheatre from which there was seemingly no egress. "And that," said Tashi, pointing ahead to its semicircular wall of mauve cliffs topped with jagged points of snow, "is the Sanju Dawan." Whereupon we knew that the Sanju Dawan was going to be a thrill, for it looked as if there were no possible way either over or through that looming wall of rock and snow.

The meadows were alive with furry little marmots sitting cockily in the sun before their holes, chattering shrilly at each other and popping in promptly when we got too close.

In a chill silvery sunset we came upon a few bleak Kirghiz yurts beside which we camped for the night. In the hillside behind the yurts were the yard-square black mouths of caves in which the Kirghiz lived or stored their goods in the coldest weather, and beside one squatted a cheery fellow in a big fur coat looking for all the world like a Brobdingnagian marmot sunning himself before his hole.

From these Kirghiz Tashi hired yaks to help us over the pass, which was too steep for the ponies to manage loaded. Yaks are comical great beasts whose acquaintance I had not renewed since my days of ABC books. They are popular on these high passes because they have better wind than ponies and are more sure-footed. At least that is what we are told in the travel books. It seemed to me more that they were so short-legged that they couldn't topple over, and even if they did they wouldn't have far enough to fall to hurt themselves or their loads.

The next morning we climbed in the cold thin sunshine, over aniline-green meadows dotted with hundreds of chattering marmots and cut by foaming glacial streams, right up to the foot of the precipitous walls. There we stopped for breath. And then didn't our Ladakhis start zigzagging agilely up that cliff like ibex, pulling, pushing, and coaxing the unladen ponies along with them. The great unruly black yaks pushed up under their own steam, careening over rocks and boulders exactly like tanks at the Front, while we panted along behind. Our hearts pounded like engines and when we stopped for breath it seemed as if there was no air at all, though a high wind was blowing.

The men were excited. *"Yakken boldi keldimur, Sanju Dawan,"* they shouted at the tops of their voices. "We're coming well, Sanju Pass."

At last we reached the top of the cliff, which we found to be a knife-edge, the descent straight down a thousand feet through a savage mass of boulders and scree and a biting gale whistling through the narrow gap over which we all tumbled breathlessly.

None of us were ill but only very breathless, with slight headaches. We had been most worried about Moses, for a Yarkandi who wanted to go with us as cook had assured us, as Owen rendered it, that "Fattish men of forty blow up and die on a high pass." But he came over gallantly.

CHAPTER XVI. *Of more stupendous mountains,
including remarks on yaks and on sensations at
18,300 feet above the sea.*

FROM the Sanju to the Suget Pass was a jumble of days through weird Gargantuan valleys, fording and re-fording the Karakash, River of Black Jade, with the green water swirling about our saddle flaps, past the ruins of a robber-captain's fortress, threading the somber Shahidulla gorge, and at last coming to Suget Karaul, the farthest military outpost of the Chinese, a small mud-walled compound where all caravans must be inspected and taxes, of course, collected. The officer in charge entertained us with gossip and tea while our men haggled over taxes, and presented us with two live chickens. Tashi came in greatly excited to say that the inspectors were forcing him to buy grain from them at their own price but that he already had plenty. It sounded rather like a hold-up, and Owen asked the officer to let him off, but later we bitterly regretted interfering, when shortage of grain forced us to double up on some of the most difficult marches of the journey.

Below the Suget (17,616 feet) we camped in the snow

and we climbed across it in a swirling snowstorm, the men nervous and muttering Tibetan prayers.

Next came the highest pass of all, the Karakoram, 18,310 feet. It is nearly a mile higher than the highest mountain in the United States, but it certainly doesn't look it, as there are no glaciers to cross and the approach to it is gradual, up wide bare wind-swept valleys, brassy under a harsh blue sky, and with herds of Tibetan antelope scuttling along the foot of the hills. Even with the sights of his rifle broken Owen shot plenty for the pot. Tashi had broken the sights coming down the Sanju and I had stuck them on, inaccurately, with adhesive tape, so that he was apt to aim at a buck and ignominiously hit a doe.

One night we camped beside a heap of abandoned bales of Indian hemp which some unfortunate caravan had tried to get to India but had had to leave behind, probably because it had been caught in a storm and lost too many ponies. We had passed many similar piles, usually Indian hemp or bales of felts. The hemp is used to make hashish and is very valuable, but even with these precious bales it seems to be an unwritten law among the caravans to leave them unmolested until their owner can return the following season to retrieve them. Our Tashi would occasionally dash off the road, disappear behind a rock in a whole sea of rocks and bob out with a pair of shoes or a bit of old felt which he had cached on some previous journey.

288

Turkestan Reunion

Much more conspicuous than abandoned loads along these bleak ways were the carcasses of dead animals which lined them in all stages of decay, from fresh corpses on which the ravens had just begun to feast to the bleached bones of seasons long gone by. We had begun to see, and smell, them soon after leaving Sanju, and they had become more and more numerous as the grazing dwindled to nothing and the way climbed higher. They were always thickest around the springs where we must camp and the stench was often so terrific that we could scarcely bear it.

We went to bed the next night in a yellow valley between red hills and woke at dawn to find it white, our camp buried in snow and snow drifted into our tent to lay a white blanket over our sleeping-bags. The caravan men never used a tent, but would stack the loads in a semicircular wall against the wind and sleep in its lee, often lying for warmth in the ashes of the supper fire.

Whenever it stormed we would urge Moses to sleep in our tent but he would never consent. "These men have good tempers," he would say, "and so you trust them, but they are not like us and how do you know that they might not decamp with your loads in the night?"

That day we met a caravan from Ladakh, the leader of which was Tashi's brother. They embraced each other. He gave Tashi some Tibetan roasted meal. Tashi gave him an antelope's head which Owen had discarded, and

289

they passed on, to meet perhaps six months later on the same road. Two trips are as much as they can make in a year, one in the spring and one in the autumn, for in winter the snows are too great and in summer the rivers are too deep to ford.

In the evening we camped in a rocky cul-de-sac of the hills, sheltered from the wind but stinking with corpses. I had a headache and couldn't breathe inside the tent. Neither of us could sleep except in a sitting position.

We were wakened in the pitch dark. I suppose it was about midnight, though our watches had long been out of commission. The wind had died down and Owen held a candle while the men loaded the ponies and we gulped a cup of tea. Our lanterns and flashlights had long since been broken and we were traveling over this way of blizzards with nothing to light us but candles. It was bitter cold and I had fortunately unpacked my Siberian felt boots before we went to bed. Owen walked to keep warm but I was far too short of breath. The men were evidently considering this crossing of the Karakoram an ordeal, and so it proved to be.

After what seemed like an age of picking our way in the frigid dark, dawn came at last and the promise of warmth to our numb feet, revealing a Styx-like landscape of weird bare hills, with huge black ravens gorged heavy on caravan carrion hovering and flapping like thunderclouds over our heads. We were climbing steadily until when, turning into a narrower valley, we came to the last slope of this highest of all our passes, it looked only like a little hill. By this time the path was lined thickly with skeletons and the corpses of ponies stiffened gruesomely into contortions of death. Some of them had been half-eaten by wolves, though we saw only ravens, sinister ravens forever flapping overhead and taunting our weary ponies with a threat of black-winged immortality.

It was a grim little hill in the cold dawn (Karakoram means Black Gravel), until, as we slanted up it, the sun peered over a rim and turned it yellow. At the top we rested beside a cairn marking the spot where Andrew Dalgleish, a Scotchman, had been murdered by a Pathan in the eighties.

The Karakoram Pass supposedly marks the vague limits of Chinese territory, but Moses was the least moved of us all about that.

Over the pass the road sloped down into a vast sun-filled valley, smooth and bare and shining with all the colors of a nasturtium bed, the only signs of life a far-away herd of Tibetan antelope gleaming in the slanting rays of the early morning sun.

As the sun mounted we removed layers of clothing, and by noon we were hot. We ate lunch at a bare camping ground and were ready to stop for the day, for we had already traveled a long hard stage. But the caravan had plodded far ahead and we had to follow.

Turkestan Reunion

In the middle of the afternoon we came to a spring in a dry river bed where a large caravan of pilgrims were camped. They were brewing tea over a tiny fire nursed carefully with bits of fuel they had brought on their ponies, and they invited us to stop. They were several families of Turki who had been on pilgrimage to Mecca and were on their way home. Some of them had been traveling for two years and were returning weather-beaten but sanctified, to be the revered heroes of their villages for the rest of their lives.

Ever since we had left Sanju Bazaar we had met pilgrims on the road, sometimes two or three parties of them in a day, mounted on scarlet-blanketed ponies with gaily striped saddle bags slung behind their high saddles. Most of them were returning poor, for it took the savings of a lifetime for a Turki to travel to Mecca. If they were able to bring a treasure home from their travels it was inevitably an umbrella bought in an Indian bazaar, and slung from the saddle, or a pair of spectacles proudly worn, the larger the better.

It was always thrilling to meet travelers on that barren road. And as soon as we spied them we prayed that they might have a few Indian rupees stowed somewhere about their persons. *"Rupee bar ma?"* we would shout at them after we had exchanged salaams. *"Rupee yok,"* they would usually call back, but occasionally one would dig deep into his clothes or saddle bags and produce one or two or three Indian coins, for which we would give him an equal number of *ak-tenga* or Turkestan half-taels. The occasion for all this petty bartering being that in Turkestan there are no banks, and having been caught at our departure with a surplus of Turkestan coins, our only means of getting rid of them was to exchange them with travelers along the way. We had bought what rupees we could find in Kashgar and Yarkand, but the rest had to be acquired by ones or twos. We made quite a haul from the caravan on the Karakoram. While the women served us tea the men dug into their bags and money-belts and brought their little store to Owen, who sat cross-legged on the sand counting out little piles of *ak-tengas* to match their piles of rupees. We changed several hundred along the road this way but we still have little packages of them stowed in our luggage which we may be able to sell to museums or coin collectors.

We said good-by to the pilgrims and set off, somewhat refreshed, after our caravan, which we hoped to find camped around each bend. But we plodded on and on and on to the next spring where caravans camped, and still they were not there. This spring was called Daulat Beg Uldi, which means "Daulat Beg Died (Here)" and we didn't blame him. By this time I was having to dismount every mile or so to rest, and we vowed that never again would we let our caravan men get so far ahead that we couldn't stop them. We knew that their idea was to keep on until they dropped on these barren grassless stages in order to get down sooner to a little grazing, and they were perfectly pleased to risk killing us all with fatigue in order to save a day's rations of grain for the ponies. As a matter of fact they had figured so closely on the grain they carried, planning to do these grassless stages quickly, that we couldn't have camped sooner without risk of losing our transport, so that it was by the grace of God that we pulled through without mishap.

Around a bend in the road we came upon Tashi lying fast asleep. He too was exhausted but encouraged us with the news that camp was not far off. We staggered through a short pass in the bare hills and came up into sunset on a wide plateau, the famous Depsang Plain, nearly 17,000 feet above sea-level and edged with little sugar-cones which are the tops of some of the highest mountains in the world. To our right across the plain was K2, second only to Everest in height and yet scarcely looming above this high plateau. There was our little tent pitched in the center of its vastness, and Moses cooking supper.

From sheer weariness we got a little sleep that night, half sitting up, and the next day we pushed on and on again, another long stage and a half, for we didn't have the heart to stop the hungry ponies short of grass, but grew madder, as we grew wearier, at Tashi for not having brought more grain. It was a stupendous day, but somehow I stood it better than the last, for instead of the weary blankness of the Karakoram the way was a series of exciting surprises, deep red gorges, winding river beds, and finally a steep savage valley into which we climbed over a giant mass of débris which had fallen from the mountain tops.

The lower we descended from the Karakoram the higher seemed the mountains all about us, until, teetering for several hours up and down the steep cliff sides of the Murgo gorge, we zigzagged dizzily down into a more stupendous and eerie mountain fastness than I had ever dreamed of. It was a terrific meeting of giant gorges spilling out from between colossal jagged peaks, a rough rim of pink snows and violet glaciers shading quickly down into deep red and purple, and with a great noise of rushing water in its black depths, an immensity fearsome enough for the oldest, greatest gods.

In the twilight we stumbled down the last rocky slope to camp on a damp fan of arsenic-green moss slapped in patches of wet plush on the moist black earth. After our long dry days of red and yellow, nothing had ever looked so wet or so green or so black. There was no other growing thing than the oozing turf and it was all very eerie and unreal. Soon the looming peaks close about us faded into black darkness and the waterfalls roared a great crescendo till we fell into heavy sleep.

CHAPTER XVII. *Of murder in Panamik and how my husband lived up to being a white man. Of finding tourists in Leh and the sadness of becoming tourists.*

A SHORT march down to the Shayok River unfolded more stupendous panorama but was pale after Bulak-i-Murgo. Beyond the Shayok, however, we crossed the most thrillingly beautiful of the five high passes, the Sasser Dawan, 17,500 feet.

From a putrid corpse-strewn camp among rocks we climbed quickly into ice and snow and up over a marvelous blue-white glittering glacier, prodding the ice with our sticks to find a footing. At the very top we met some Hajjis on yaks with whom we swapped a few rupees, and then slipped and slithered down an icy slope to a jungle of tumbled rocks over which we clambered for hours with the sparkling cathedral peaks looming all about us.

The day before I had developed a riding strain which made mounting and dismounting very painful and climbing over rocks almost equally so, but Tashi stuck by me all day, cheerfully helping me over the hardest bits and tootling his flute whenever we stopped for rest. At last we came down to unhealthy-looking green turf and plashing streamlets and camped where there was yak-dung for fuel.

The next day a back-breaking march brought us to the Nubra valley and signs of human habitation at long last. First, high on the cliffs of a prodigious rocky valley, we passed solitary shepherds with vast flocks of goats and sheep, and then, in the late afternoon, on a narrow ledge over a plunging river, the camp of a small gang of road-menders.

Over the Karakoram we had kept on for the sake of the ponies, and here it was for the sake of the men. For their homes were in the Nubra valley and if they could only get us far enough they could spend the night at home. So instead of camping we climbed another pass. It didn't count as one of the five, but it might well have, straight up five hundred feet and straight down a thousand, down into the green valley of the Nubra, on the banks of which we camped, the men scampering off as soon as the supper fires were built to see their families and friends and herald our coming.

So the next morning when we rode into the leafy lanes of Panamik, their village, we were met by the headman, in a purple robe and riding a gaily caparisoned horse, and at the first group of little white cottages the family of our youngest pony man were all lined up to greet us with offerings of flowers and *chang*. *Chang* is a flat kind of barley beer, which they offered to us in wooden bowls lined with beaten silver.

The headman led the way on his black pony. He wore a kind of peaked red hat and one large turquoise earring, and when the villagers saw us coming they all came out of their toy houses to watch us pass. The women wore red cobra-shaped headdresses, pointed in front, with the tail down their backs, and sewed all over with bits of turquoise, furry flaps over their ears, and a goatskin hanging from their shoulders.

We filed through several miles of leafy lanes lined with willows and poplars and rose bushes heavy with crimson haws, and little babbling irrigation ditches. Every little while the path would widen out on either side of a *mani* wall or pass by tall white *chortens*. A *mani* wall is a long flat-topped stone wall covered with slabs of rock on which prayers are carved, the *"om mani padme hum"* of the lamas, and which pious souls always pass on their right. A *chorten* is what we call in Peking a *dagoba,* a monument to the dead, fat at the bottom and topped with a needle spire, like a kind of top we had as children which spun with a string.

Behind thorny hedges and stone walls nestled little white farmhouses and every few hundred yards would be a tiny hamlet of white plastered houses lining the narrow flag-stoned road, flat-roofed with tiny windows and carved wood balconies. Some of the houses had two or three stories and looked quite palatial in comparison with the grandest houses of Turkestan, but we found on further residence in Panamik that even those with the most impressive Queen Anne fronts had decidedly Mary Ann interiors. Their entire ground floor was given over to the cows, sheep, goats and chickens, from which messy stable one ascended by a rickety ladder to a sort of loft where the family and minor pets ate and slept, a supply of dung for fuel being stored in the corners.

Tsetan Bai, the headman, who was also the owner of our caravan, led us to a green meadow on the edge of the village where we camped happily for several days, the headman lavishly supplying us with eggs, chickens, and milk, and inviting us at frequent intervals to join his family circle round their kitchen fire for tea and *chang*. The family was large and we never did get it all quite straight. Our handsomest pony man was a son-in-law. There seemed to be numerous sons-in-law, as most Ladakhi women have several husbands. The children were even more smiling and grubby than their parents and dressed like them in coarse wool and matted fur and much silver and turquoise.

The tea, which we drank from silver bowls, was stewed thick and black, with flavoring of salt and rancid butter and the option of thickening it with roasted flour stirred with a finger and gulped down as porridge. The *chang* was thin and cool and refreshing. Their room was low, the mud walls and thatched ceiling black from years of smoke. The fire was on a low platform; over it hung a huge iron cauldron, and behind it were a few crude copper bowls and kettles and a row of wood and silver cups. The wrinkled and toothless old wife of the headman hung like a witch over her cauldron. We made the grown-ups presents of cakes of scented soap and the headman promptly bought in the full supply. Other presents we made more privately, but the headman probably got them all in the end, as he was rich and greedy. We had good reason later to know that he was greedy for he escorted us on to Leh himself with the scratchiest lot of transport you can imagine.

When we weren't visiting Tsetan Bai half Panamik was visiting us, too enthralled with our queer belongings and our queerer ways to tend to their harvesting. Several other caravans were camping about the village, and at dark little supper fires here and there beneath the trees lit up circles of brown faces, pilgrims and merchants resting from their long arduous travels.

One night we had an adventure. We were just starting to bed when we heard a great noise of shouting in the village and, curiosity overcoming our caravan custom of early to bed, we stumbled up the rocky path to see what it was all about. Halfway toward the center of the village we met two acquaintances tearing for dear life down the hill. They stopped us. *"Yaman, yaman!* Don't go up there! Very big fight, caravan man killed!"

Following the din we came to a great crowd of shouting, gesticulating men in a courtyard. We pushed in, and Owen, assuming a white man's rôle, demanded to know what the row was all about. And where was the dead man? Over there, lying where he had fallen in a far corner of the yard. Owen, with an air of boldness which he didn't feel, walked over and felt of his heart. It was still beating, and Ladakhis and Turkis crowded around, one sturdy caravan leader with a very battered bleeding head. *"Inshallah!* He is not dead! But very unconscious. What should be done?"

"Turn him over and put a pillow under his head, and let me know when he wakes up," Owen directed, and we stalked off home, where we hastily looked up "Concussion" in our first-aid book. Fortunately the book approved of our simple prescription, so we went to bed in peace, the village seeming to have done likewise.

The next morning the "corpse" was still unconscious and the other caravan man's head still covered with clotted blood. Owen offered to bathe and bandage him but he seemed to want to keep all his evidence on him till the case was settled.

In the meantime Owen, who was thoroughly enjoying being thrust into the rôles of physician and judge, demanded to see the "murderers." The chief culprit had fled into the hills, but two others had been locked up by the headman and were produced. Owen took their pictures, then photographed the "corpse," and threatened, if the man died, to take them all to Leh to see the District Commissioner. His caravan companions wanted to sling him, still unconscious, onto the back of a horse and take him on, to be well out of difficulties, but this Owen sternly forbade.

About noon he came to, and at intervals all afternoon the caravan sent delegations to ask Owen if they might not start. By this time we were very mirthful over Owen's "court" and the solemn conclaves which gathered about our tent, but continued outwardly stern, and finally, after applying large quantities of iodine to "murdered" and "murderers" alike and administering rations of aspirin he pronounced the corpse well enough to travel. Since the caravan showed not the least desire for retribution or revenge we judged that both sides were doubtless equally to blame.

The next day we too left Panamik escorted by Tsetan Bai and several oafish villagers, and only Tashi of our former caravan men. We still had before us the last of the five high passes, the Khardong, 17,400 feet, and it proved the most exciting and difficult of them all. For a day and a half we followed peacefully from village to village down the Nubra valley to its fork with the Shayok, then up the Shayok, whose high banks were covered with débris, brought down by a great spate of a year or so before which had carried away the bridge and took us far out of our way to find a ford.

Evening brought us to a *serai* at a high bare little hamlet where there was a congestion of caravans waiting for yaks to help them over the Khardong pass. Loads were stacked as high as the walls and some of the caravan men said they had been waiting there for weeks. Tsetan Bai managed some way to do a dicker which produced yaks for us the very next morning.

At the foot of the pass we made a chill and barren camp among desolate gray rocks, where we had only melted snow for water and scant bits of dung for fuel and where we could only keep a little warm by crawling inside our sleeping bags.

From a piercing cold before-the-dawn start we climbed straight up over rocks to the snow and soon came to the foot of a steep slide of ice. Several hundred yards almost straight above us we saw a line of black specks which proved to be unladen yaks returning to the *serai*. At the top of the ice slide the men headed each one down and gave it a great push, whereupon it braced itself sturdily and slid down like a toboggan, recovering its balance at the bottom just in time to save itself a fall over a cliff.

It took us hours to get up that slide that the yaks had slid down so spryly. It was so steep and slippery that it seemed almost impossible to find a foothold and much of the way we crawled on our hands and knees. The sturdy old yaks had to be unloaded and their loads hauled up with ropes and one of the yaks had to be tugged up the slipperiest slope.

I reached the top first as I wasn't bothering about loads and Owen had stopped to take photographs. After ploughing across a glacier covered with deep soft snow I found a ledge of rock somewhat sheltered from the icy wind from which I could see the world laid out for me in two directions. The way we had come was a mass of ice and rock stretching steeply down between two walls of jagged mountains, and I could watch our black caravan slowly laboring up. In the other direction the way that we were going stretched steeply down to a far-away green valley in the midst of which I could distinguish the castles and *chorten* spires of Leh, the capital of Ladakh. Beyond Leh stretched a silver ribbon, the Indus River, and beyond the Indus was a breath-taking sight, range after range of the snowy high Himalayas.

I watched our yaks lurching through the soft glacier snow to the summit of the pass, stop a few minutes to rest, and then start barging down toward Leh. Owen joined me in my eyrie and we lingered there as long as we dared, loath to start down from the last of the high passes of Central Asia.

For we knew that in Leh we would find the beginnings of civilization and a traveled road. And so it proved, for while we are still half a month from Kashmir and India, Leh's *dak* bungalow, post office and telegraph office spell the beginning of the end. There are even tourists here, a German novelist, an artist, and a Harvard student. They looked at Owen's red beard and our patched little tent and asked us where we had come from. But they simply didn't believe it when we said "Peking."

MAPS

The following pages contain facsimile reproductions of the original map art that appeared in the 1930 edition of Owen Lattimore's *High Tartary*. The place names have changed over the years—for fuller information, consult the table of names on pp. 315–318.

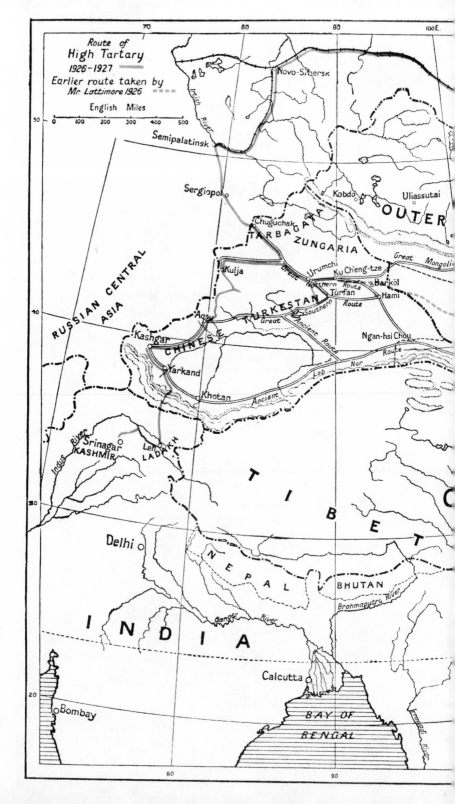

Route of
High Tartary
1926-1927
Earlier route taken by
Mr. Lattimore 1926

English Miles
0   100   200   300   400   500

Novo-Sibirsk

Semipalatinsk

Sergiopol

Kobdo

Uliassutai

OUTER

Chuguchak

TARBA GAI

ZUNGARIA

Great

Mongoli

Kulja

Urumchi

Ku Chieng-tze

Barköl

Northern Route

Turfan

Hami

TURKESTAN

Southern Route

Aqsu

Great

Ancient Route

Kashgar

CHINESE

Ngan-hsi Chou

Yarkand

Nor Route

Lob

Khotan

Ancient

Indus River

Srinagar

KASHMIR

Leh

LADAKH

TIBET

Delhi

NEPAL

BHUTAN

Brahmaputra River

Ganges River

INDIA

Calcutta

Bombay

BAY OF
BENGAL

Irrawaddy River

RUSSIAN CENTRAL ASIA

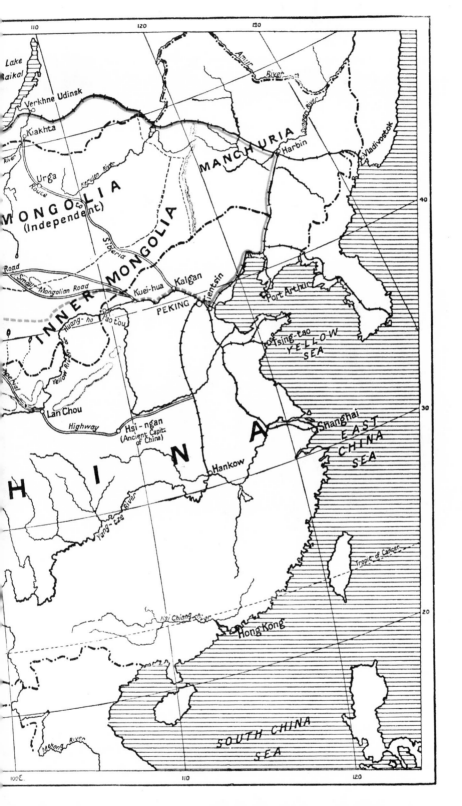

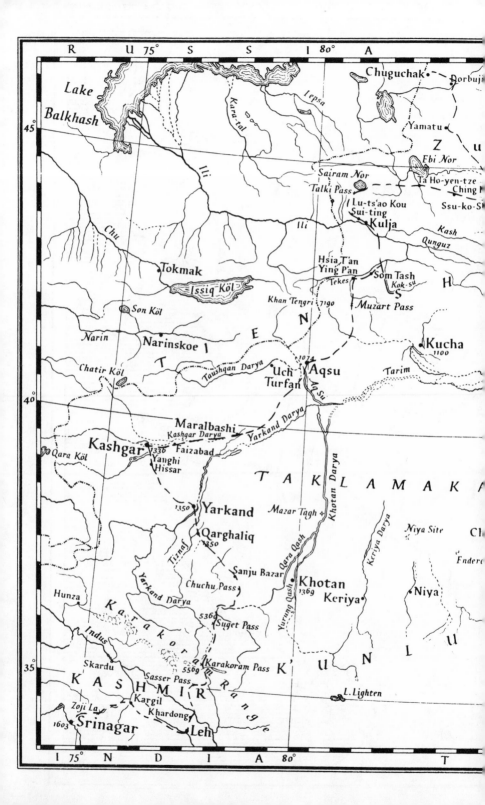

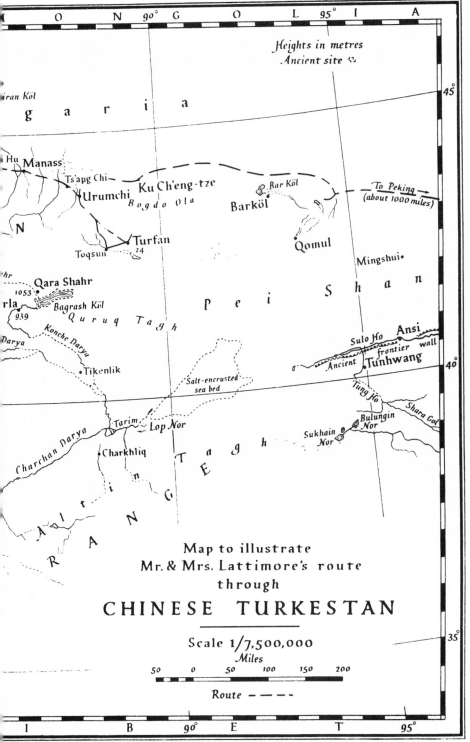

Map to illustrate
Mr. & Mrs. Lattimore's route
through

CHINESE TURKESTAN

Scale 1/7,500,000

Miles

50   0   50   100   150   200

Route - - - - -

C. Denny, del.

A WORD ABOUT PROPER NAMES

In the 1920s when Eleanor Lattimore wrote *Turkestan Reunion*, there was no clear standardization for usage or Western spellings of names of Turkic, Mongol or other Central Asian peoples and places. The usages adopted by Eleanor and Owen Lattimore have been kept in this volume, but since some of these have long since fallen out of fashion or favor, we add here a short chart of some modern-day equivalents:

Usage in *Turkestan Reunion*	Pinyin Usage	Other Common Usage
Bakti		Bakhty
Barkul (ponies)	Balikun	Barkol
Bogdo Shan (Holy Mountains)	Bogeda Shan	Bogda Shan
Cathay		(North) China
Changchun		Hsinking
Chantos		Turkis, Uygurs
Chihli	Zhili, Hebei	Hopeh
Chinese Turkestan	Xinjiang	Sinkiang

A Word About Proper Names

Ching Ho	Jing He	
Chuguchak	Tacheng	T'a-Ch'eng
Dawandung	Dabancheng	Ta-pan-ch'eng
Eleuths		Ölöts
Faizabad	Jiashi	Payzawat, Ch'ich-Shih
Fire Mountains	Huoshan	
Harbin	Haerbin	Kharbin, Ha-erh-pin
Ho Shang	Heshang	
Hsi Hu	Xi Hu	
Ili	Ili	I-li
Jenghis Khan		Genghis Khan, Qinggis Khan
Kalgan	Zhangjiakou	Chang-chia-K'ou
Kansu	Gansu	
Kara Kitai		(Hsi) Liao
Karaksh	Moyu	Qara Qash, Karakax
Karakorum		K'a-la'k'un-lun
Kargalik	Yecheng	Qarghaliq, Yeh-ch'eng
Kashgar	Kashi	K'a-shih
Kazak		Kazakh, Qazaq
Khotan	Hotan	Ho-t'ien

A Word About Proper Names

Koksu		Kök-su
Kucha	Kuche	K'u-ch'e
Kueihua	Guihua,	Huhhot,
	Huhehaode	Huhehot
Kuen Lun	Kunlun	K'un-lun
Kulja	Yining	I-ning
Lop Nor	Loulan Yiji	Lo-pu Po
Manass	Manasi	Ma-na-ssu Ho
Manchuli	Manzhouli	Man-chou Li
Manchus	Manzhou	
Maralbashi	Bachu	Pa-ch'u
Mukden	Shenyang	Shen-yang
Muzart Pas	Muzhati	Muzat He
North Road	Beilu	Pei-lu
Panamik		Panimikh
Peking	Beijing	
Posgam	Zepu	
Qum Ariq River		Aksu He
Sairam Nor		Sai-li-mu Hu,
		Sayram Hu
Sanju		Sang-chu-pa-
		cha
Shansi	Shanxi	Shan-hsi
Shensi	Shaanxi	Shan-hsi
Sinkiang	Xinjiang	
South Road	Nanlu	
Suget Pass		Su-kai-t'i

317

A Word About Proper Names

Sui Ting	Suiding	
Sze Tai		Ssu-t'ai
Taklamakan desert	Taklimakan Shamo	T'a-k'o-la makan Sha-mo
Tarim		Tarim Pendi, T'a-li-mu P'en-ti
Tatar		Tartar
Tekkes Valley	Tekesi	T'e-k'o-ssu
Tien Shan (Heavenly Mountains)	Tianshan	
Tientsin	Tianjin	T'ien-chin
Toksun	Tuokexun	T'o-k'o-hsün
T'o Li		T'o-lai
T'ung-kan		Dungan
Turfan		T'u-lu-fan, Turpan
Uigurs		Uygur
Urumchi		Tihwa, Wu-lu-mu-ch'i, Ürümqi
Yarkand	Shache	Ya-erh-ch'iang, So-ch'e
Zungaria	Junggaria	Dzungaria, Chun-ka-erh P'en-ti, Junggaria

BIOGRAPHICAL NOTE
David Lattimore

My mother, Eleanor Holgate Lattimore (1895–1970), was the first American woman to travel overland from Beijing—called "Peking" in those days—to India, trekking from oasis to oasis and crossing the high wastes of Turkestan (Kazakhstan and Xinjiang), in the heart of the Asian continent. This was in 1926 and 1927. There was, at that time, no "night train to Turkestan," to quote the title of a more recent travel narrative. Eleanor and her husband journeyed in the traditional ways of the country: by camel caravan and horse-drawn sledge, in jolting pony carts, and on ponyback, with yaks to tote the baggage at high altitudes.

Turkestan Reunion is my mother's story of this pioneering, often idyllic, sometimes desperately difficult wedding journey, the hardest parts of which the bride and groom carried out separately, for reasons she explains in her book. The book consists of letters that Eleanor wrote home to her family in Evanston, Illinois. That, however, doesn't fully account for her reassuring breeziness, which came from deep within her personality.

Eleanor's parents were Canadians. Her father started his life's work as a village schoolmaster in Ontario, became an authority on analytic geometry, and served a remarkable thirty-one years as Dean of the College of Liberal Arts at Northwestern University; for five of those years he was also the university's president *ad interim*. The other family members to whom Eleanor addressed her letters included her mother and sister Tim, both of whom remained housebound with tuberculosis for much of their lives, and another sister, Barbara, a divorced YWCA executive who had returned home with a small child.

Despite these and other reasons for grief, Eleanor's family had provided her with an enormously nurturing and idealistic—although restrictive—milieu in which to grow up. To this she owed both her self-confidence and her rebellious streak. After college she didn't, as she had once vowed, become a missionary; rather, she spent the years of World War I visiting army bases, where she persuaded runaway girls—"camp followers," as they were called—to return to their homes. Later she helped to establish the YWCA in Estonia, and returned to China, where she had traveled earlier when her father was on sabbatical. Her ambitions to explore and to write had been spurred by her friendship with the romantic

Biographical Note

radical Rayna Simons, the muse of Vincent Sheean and Dorothy Day.

In Beijing Eleanor met and married my father, Owen Lattimore, a young American businessman who had scholarly interests, very little money, and a yen to retrace ancient trade routes. My father's linguistic gifts and deep knowledge of China combined with my mother's buoyant drive and the wiliness of their Chinese servant, Moses, were sufficient to carry off successfully their shoestring journey together—a journey that might have foundered at many points across a supposedly "closed" country landlocked by mighty mountains, deserts, and steppes.

Besides *Turkestan Reunion* the journey resulted in two books by my father, *The Desert Road to Turkestan* (1928, 1929) and *High Tartary* (1930). Speaking for myself, I am delighted that Kodansha America is reissuing these early works by my parents. In rereading them, I have been charmed, not only by the old stories remembered but also by the books' innocent ebullience and by their lightly worn literacy. Though perhaps I am not the one to say so, I suspect that these are among the best narratives that came out of the great flowering of travel writing in the first three or four decades of the century.

In later years, Eleanor collaborated with Owen in writing *The Making of Modern China* (1944) and its revised version, *China: A Short History* (1947), and in compiling

Biographical Note

an anthology, *Silks, Spices, and Empire* (1968), subtitled *Asia Through the Eyes of Its Discoverers*. These, at any rate, were the books they signed jointly. In fact, she inspired and edited all of his many books, with the one exception of his scholarly magnum opus, *Inner Asian Frontiers of China* (1940, 1951). As Owen gladly admitted, she was the driving force behind his academic and journalistic careers and behind his defense from the likes of Senator Joseph McCarthy during the period of shameful demagoguery through which our country passed after the "fall" of China (1949) and the Korean debacle. *Turkestan Reunion* was the only book wholly her own. Some might say that, having escaped from one benign academic panjandrum, her father, she ended, a bit ironically, by submerging her own career in that of another academic eminence, my father. Whether she should or could have chosen differently I do not know. The effort took its toll. After her too-early death, my father never found anyone to match her.

I like to think of them in the glory of their youth, fording together the flooded Tekes River, as Owen described it in *High Tartary*:

> After a few strides the ponies were swept off their feet and carried rapidly down-river. I looked at my wife, and saw her laughing; I felt under me the gallant effort of Iskander, swimming freely, and

Biographical Note

my heart rose to it. The savage yelling of the Qazaqs
rose to a frantic pitch; but it was not frantic, for
they too were laughing boldly, and they too were
exulting in the struggle and the sense of contest, in
the courage of their ponies and their own skill.
(p. 248)

David Lattimore
Lincoln, Massachusetts
October, 1994

KODANSHA GLOBE

International in scope, this series offers distinguished books that explore the lives, customs, and mindsets of peoples and cultures around the world.

MAN MEETS DOG
Konrad Lorenz
Illustrated by Konrad Lorenz
  and Annie Eisenmenger
New introduction by
  Donald McCaig
Translated by
  Marjorie Kerr Wilson
1-56836-051-7

**SARAJEVO, EXODUS OF
A CITY**
Dzevad Karahasan
Afterword by
  Slavenka Drakulić
Translated by
  Slobodan Drakulić
1-56836-057-6

MERCHANT PRINCES
*An Intimate History
  of Jewish Families
  Who Built Great
  Department Stores*
Leon Harris
New introduction by
  Kenneth Libo
New foreword by
  Oscar Handlin
1-56836-044-4

**THE FORBIDDEN
EXPERIMENT**
*The Story of the Wild
  Boy of Aveyron*
Roger Shattuck
New introduction by
  Douglas Keith Candland
1-56836-048-7

TURKESTAN REUNION
Eleanor Holgate
  Lattimore
Illustrations by Eleanor
  Frances Lattimore
1-56836-053-3

HIGH TARTARY
Owen Lattimore
Original photographs by
  Owen Lattimore
New introduction by
  Orville Schell
1-56836-054-1

GOD'S LAUGHTER
*Physics, Religion, and
  the Cosmos*
Gerhard Staguhn
1-56836-045-2

**THE FOUR-CORNERED
FALCON**
*Essays on the Interior
  West and the Natural
  Scene*
Reg Saner
1-56836-049-5

THE CROSSING PLACE
*A Journey Among the
  Armenians*
Philip Marsden
New introduction by
  Peter Sourian
1-56836-052-5

TRACING IT HOME
A Chinese Journey
Lynn Pan
1-56836-043-6

**TRESPASSERS ON THE
ROOF OF THE WORLD**
*The Secret Exploration
  of Tibet*
Peter Hopkirk
1-56836-050-9

To order, contact your local bookseller or call 1-800-788-6262 (mention code G1). For a complete listing of titles, please contact the Kodansha Editorial Department at Kodansha America, Inc., 114 Fifth Avenue, New York, NY 10011.